Socialist and Labor Songs

An International Revolutionary Songbook

Socialist and Labor Songs

An International

Revolutionary Songbok

Edited by
Elizabeth Morgan

Preface by
Utah Phillips

The Charles H. Kerr Library

PM Press

Socialist and Labor Songs: An International Revolutionary Songbook
Edited by Elizabeth Morgan

PM Press
PO Box 23912
Oakland, CA 94623
www.pmpress.org

Published in conjunction with the Charles H. Kerr Publishing Company
C.H. Kerr Company
1726 Jarvis Avenue
Chicago, IL 60626
www.charleshkerr.com

Cover design by Josh MacPhee/justseeds.org/antumbradesign.org
Layout by Jonathan Rowland

ISBN: 978-1-60486-392-5
Library of Congress Control Number: 2013911526

10 9 8 7 6 5 4 3 2

Printed in the USA

CONTENTS

PREFACE

by Utah Phillips

Several years ago I had the privilege of performing at the Inn at Celo, North Carolina. While there I was taken to meet an extraordinary gentleman named Ernest Morgan. During our visit, Mr. Morgan showed me the manuscript of a songbook, the one you now hold in your hand, completed in 1958 by Elizabeth Morgan, his wife. Elizabeth Morgan was an enormously talented and energetic woman, who, besides being a fine musician and singer, was also a progressive educator and a deeply committed social and political activist. By the time of her death in 1971, her achievements were great, but the manuscript of songs so patiently compiled remained unpublished.

There I stood in Mr. Morgan's house, with this precious collection in my hands, turning page after page of treasures. Some greeted me as old friends: Harry McClintock's "Hallelujah, I'm a Bum" or Joe Hill's "The Preacher and the Slave." Only recently I had been leading participants in a homeless rally in singing Maurice Sugar's "Soup Song." But for the most part, these songs were unknown to me; either they or I had strayed off into some parallel branch of political music and had passed each other by. I had always known of our political and social movements as singing movements, and have been continually astonished at the scope and variety of our people's music. And I am always prepared to be astonished again as I was when I first sampled Elizabeth Morgan's collection. I instinctively knew that it had to be carried through to publication, and who better to publish it than Charles H. Kerr?

It's taken a while, but here it is! These songs are like endangered species that have been restored to the present, to the land of the living. They stuck up for us long ago during dark and troubled times. Our times are dark and troubled, too, but our old songs are still here with us to see us through. Sing away!

ELIZABETH MORGAN
1910 – 1971

COMMENTS

by Elizabeth Morgan
(Written in 1964)

I should like to say a little about my getting into socialist music activity. The person who got me started on it was Caroline Urie, a cousin of Lucy Morgan. She was an old Socialist who had been active in Socialist party movements in various parts of Europe and America. She was one of the early teachers of Montessori, having studied with Madam Montessori and then returned to this country to open a Montessori kindergarten at Hull House in Chicago, and had been quite a close associate of Jane Addams during the years she remained at Hull House.

At the same time that Caroline Urie was at Hull House, Eleanor Smith was there making music and these women had been very much interested in music as an expression of the struggle for better living conditions of which Hull House was one expression. Caroline Urie was a highly cultivated person and an able musician herself. She brought me music which I thoroughly respected as an art expression and from this I became interested in a much wider variety of music than just folk music.

A Socialist leader, Karl Pauli, was one of the people who happened to come to our house when I was singing some of this material and was so moved by it that he urged me to sing for conventions and various gatherings. Sam Friedman was very helpful, too.

Whenever I went on these trips I gathered more music, and some of the material was very interesting. It included music from old Bellamites that I met and sang for out in Colorado, from student radicals who had been gathering music in their own right, as well as old Wobblies and old-timers in union organizing work. I found that the United States had a very rich literature of what might be called socially conscious music, probably the richest and most varied such literature of any country in the world. Partly this is because we have inherited from all of the European countries, but to this heritage we have added some music which is really distinctive. At the time of the Second World War, Ernest and my collection of labor music was probably one of the finest private collections in the world.

I came to feel that there is rather a wide band that separates propaganda from art. While some songs originate as propaganda, they may nevertheless be good expressive songs. One of these, for example, which irritated me is "Joe Hill." "I dreamed I saw Joe Hill last night, alive as you or me." Its origin was propaganda but it has seemed to be quite an effective, living sort of song. On the other hand, some of the finest songs of American art literature have apparently been written out of deep concern. The artist, the great artist, has something to say. After exploring this kind of music, I find myself returning to more conventional forms, such as, for instance, church music, with a great deal more understanding and considerably greater sense of discrimination. I have always felt that this sort of illumination of life was worth all the struggle that I, for one, put into the Socialist movement.

THAT CAUSE

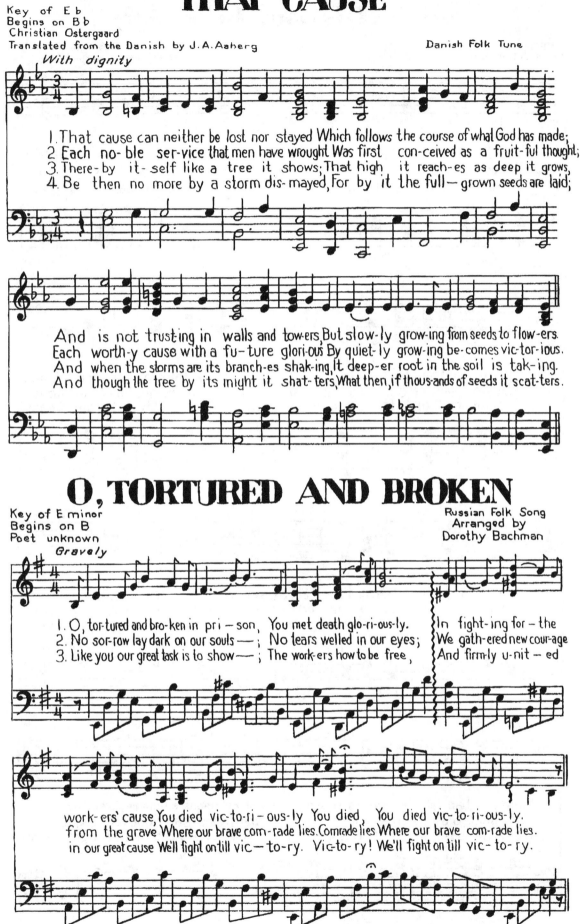

O, TORTURED AND BROKEN

Hail the Glorious Golden City

Key of F
Begins on F
Felix Adler, 1878

"Austrian Hymn"
1797, Franz Joseph Haydn

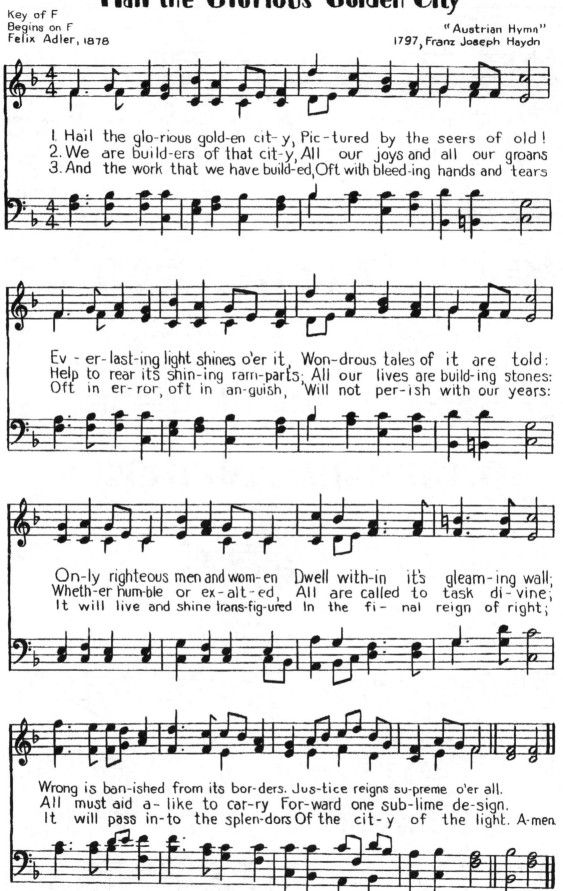

1. Hail the glo-rious gold-en cit-y, Pic-tured by the seers of old!
2. We are build-ers of that cit-y, All our joys and all our groans
3. And the work that we have build-ed, Oft with bleed-ing hands and tears

Ev - er-last-ing light shines o'er it, Won-drous tales of it are told:
Help to rear its shin-ing ram-parts; All our lives are build-ing stones:
Oft in er-ror, oft in an-guish, Will not per-ish with our years:

On-ly righteous men and wom-en Dwell with-in it's gleam-ing wall;
Wheth-er hum-ble or ex-alt-ed, All are called to task di-vine;
It will live and shine trans-fig-ured In the fi - nal reign of right;

Wrong is ban-ished from its bor-ders. Jus-tice reigns su-preme o'er all.
All must aid a-like to car-ry For-ward one sub-lime de-sign.
It will pass in-to the splen-dors Of the cit-y of the light. A-men.

MEN OF THE SOIL

Harold M. Hildreth
*With spirit but
not too fast*

"Hoesten"
(Danish harvest song)

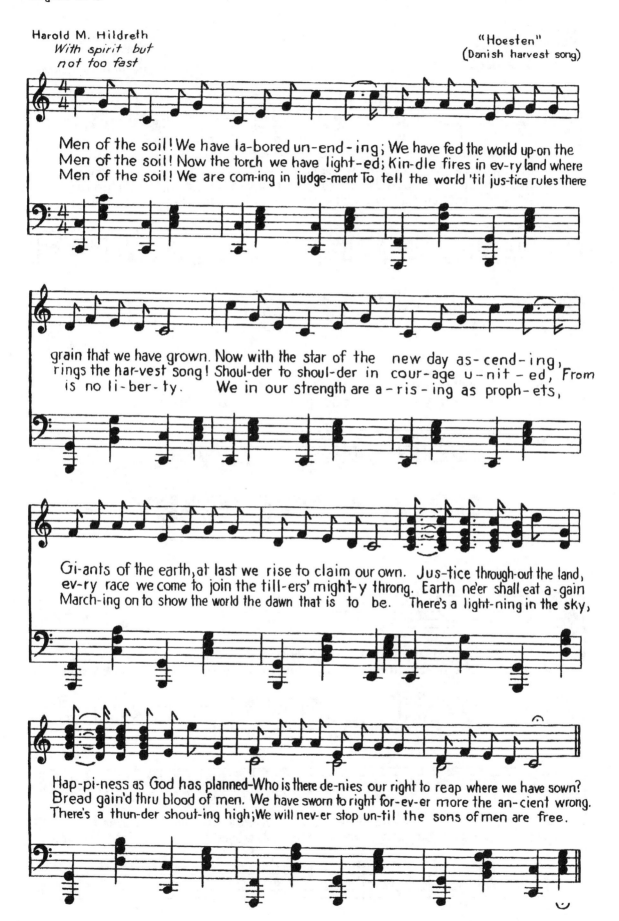

Men of the soil! We have la-bored un-end-ing; We have fed the world up-on the
Men of the soil! Now the torch we have light-ed; Kin-dle fires in ev-ry land where
Men of the soil! We are com-ing in judge-ment To tell the world 'til jus-tice rules there

grain that we have grown. Now with the star of the new day as-cend-ing,
rings the har-vest song! Shoul-der to shoul-der in cour-age u-nit-ed, From
is no li-ber-ty. We in our strength are a-ris-ing as proph-ets,

Gi-ants of the earth, at last we rise to claim our own. Jus-tice through-out the land,
ev-ry race we come to join the till-ers' might-y throng. Earth ne'er shall eat a-gain
March-ing on to show the world the dawn that is to be. There's a light-ning in the sky,

Hap-pi-ness as God has planned-Who is there de-nies our right to reap where we have sown?
Bread gain'd thru blood of men. We have sworn to right for-ev-er more the an-cient wrong.
There's a thun-der shout-ing high; We will nev-er stop un-til the sons of men are free.

WE ARE BUILDING

Key of C
Begins on E

With lower octave

"Climbing Jacob's Ladder"
Negro Spiritual
Arr. by Dorothy Bachman

1. We are build-ing a strong un-ion. We are build-ing a strong un-ion.
2. Ev-'ry new man makes us strong-er. Ev-'ry new girl makes us strong-er.
3. They have fired the men who joined us. They have fired the girls who joined us.
4. We won't budge un-til we con-quer. We will stand un-til we con-quer.

We are build-ing a strong un-ion. Work-ers in the mill.
Ev-'ry new kid makes us strong-er. Work-ers in the mill.
They have fired the kids who joined us. Work-ers in the mill.
We will fight un-til we con-quer. Work-ers in the mill.

ROCK-A-BYE, BABY

Key of A
Begins on C#

Effie Carlton

1. Rock-a-bye, ba-by, in the tree-top, When you grow up, you'll work in a shop.
2. Hush-a-bye, ba-by, in the tree-top, When you grow old, your wa-ges will stop.

When you get married, your wife will work too, So that the rich will have noth-ing to do.
When you have spent the lit-tle you've saved, Hush-a-bye, ba-by, off to the grave.

MARCH ON
In the Egypt Land

Key of F
Begins on C

Stanzas 2, 3, 4 by Samuel H. Friedman

Negro Spiritual

Allegro

1. Way o-ver in the E-gypt land, We shall gain the vic-to-ry,
2. Not on-ly on the E-gypt strand, We shall gain the vic-to-ry.
3. Wher-ev-er there's an E-gypt land, We shall gain the vic-to-ry.
4. Yes, when the work-ers un-der-stand, We shall gain the vic-to-ry.

Way o-ver in the E-gypt land, We shall gain the day.
Do Pha-raoh and his co-horts stand, We shall gain the day.
We are an ev-er grow-ing band, We shall gain the day.
They'll slave no more in E-gypt land, We shall gain the day.
} March on, and

we shall gain the vic-to-ry, March on and we shall gain the day.

MANHATTAN STREET CRIES

Key of D
Begins on A

Old English Round

Chairs to mend old chairs to mend. Mak-er-el, fresh mak-er-el. Rags, rags, an-y old rags.

CASEY JONES

Key of Bb
Begins on F
Joe Hill

"Casey Jones"

Lively

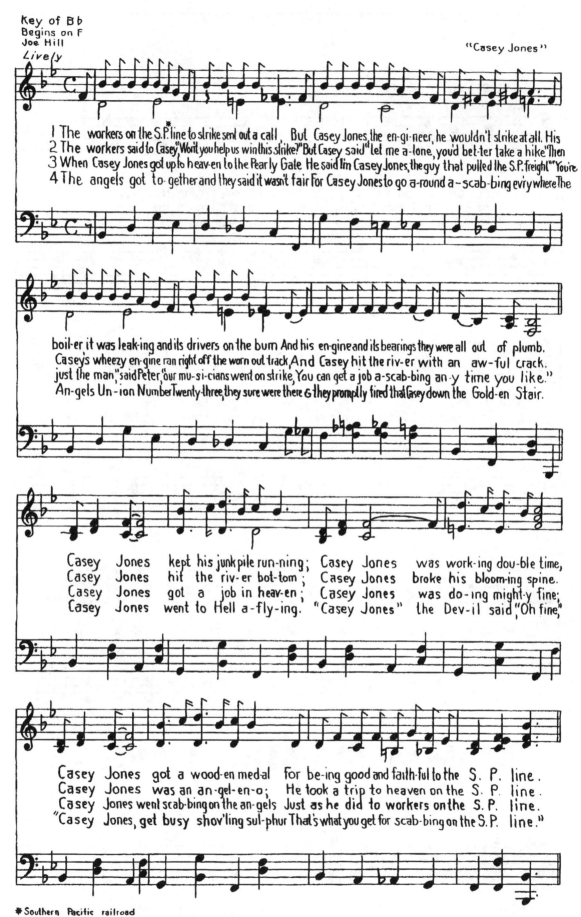

1 The workers on the S.P.* line to strike sent out a call, But Casey Jones, the en-gi-neer, he wouldn't strike at all. His
2 The workers said to Casey "Won't you help us win this strike?" But Casey said "Let me a-lone, you'd bet-ter take a hike" Then
3 When Casey Jones got up to heav-en to the Pear-ly Gate He said "I'm Casey Jones, the guy that pulled the S.P. freight" "You're
4 The angels got to-gether and they said it wasn't fair For Casey Jones to go a-round a–scab-bing evry where The

boil-er it was leak-ing and its drivers on the bum And his en-gine and its bearings they were all out of plumb.
Casey's wheezy en-gine ran right off the worn out track And Casey hit the riv-er with an aw-ful crack.
just the man" said Peter, "our mu-si-cians went on strike, You can get a job a-scab-bing an-y time you like."
An-gels Un-ion Number Twenty-three, they sure were there & they promptly fired that Casey down the Gold-en Stair.

Casey Jones   kept his junk pile run-ning; Casey Jones   was work-ing dou-ble time,
Casey Jones   hit the riv-er bot-tom; Casey Jones   broke his bloom-ing spine.
Casey Jones   got a job in heav-en; Casey Jones   was do-ing might-y fine;
Casey Jones   went to Hell a-fly-ing. "Casey Jones"   the Dev-il said "Oh fine,"

Casey Jones   got a wood-en med-al   For be-ing good and faith-ful to the S. P. line.
Casey Jones   was an an-gel-en-o;   He took a trip to heaven on the S. P. line.
Casey Jones   went scab-bing on the an-gels Just as he did to workers on the S. P. line.
"Casey Jones, get busy shov'ling sul-phur That's what you get for scab-bing on the S. P. line."

* Southern Pacific railroad

TRUE FREEDOM

Key of F
Begins on A
James Russell Lowell
With Spirit

"Hymn to Joy"
from Ninth Symphony
Ludwig van Beethoven

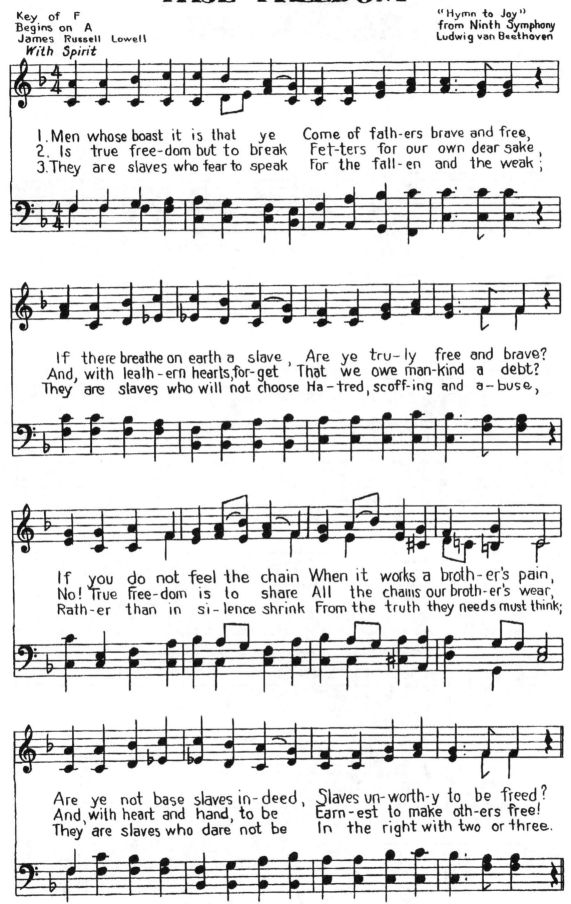

1. Men whose boast it is that ye   Come of fath-ers brave and free,
2. Is   true free-dom but to break   Fet-ters for our own dear sake,
3. They are slaves who fear to speak For the fall-en and the weak;

If there breathe on earth a slave , Are ye tru-ly free and brave?
And, with leath-ern hearts, for-get ' That we owe man-kind a debt?
They are slaves who will not choose Ha-tred, scoff-ing and a-buse,

If you do not feel the chain When it works a broth-er's pain,
No! True free-dom is to   share All the chains our broth-er's wear,
Rath-er than in si-lence shrink From the truth they needs must think;

Are ye not base slaves in-deed, Slaves un-worth-y to be freed?
And, with heart and hand, to be   Earn-est to make oth-ers free!
They are slaves who dare not be   In the right with two or three.

FUNERAL SONG
of a Russian Revolutionist

Key of C minor
Begins on G

Words adapted from Russian
by Douglas

Arrangement by
Liebich

P (Voice, calling softly)

Comrades fall in line,
preparing to start procession.

1. Pale moon de-clin-ing,
2. Lamp faint-ly gleam-ing,

grey clouds are spread-ing dark-ness a-round As sol-emn-ly we bear thee 'o'er the snow-y
hands strong and ten-der lay thee to rest And Moth-er Earth now holds thee to her chil-ly

ground. Soft winds are sigh-ing, wife, chil-dren cry-ing com-rades be-wail And na-ture's voice re-
breast. Hearts with e-mo-tion from eyes of sad-ness fast drop the tear But in in-spir-ing

sponds, with sorrow thro' the vale. Fond-ly we loved thee, thy heart true and brave
tones thy voice we seem to hear: "Weep not, my com-rades, re-mem-ber, ye brave, The

Speaks once a-gain from the brink of the grave: (soft)"Weep not in sor-row, think of the mor-row,
pris-on is strong-er by far than the grave; (loud)-Death can not hold me, still I will fol-low,

en-ter the strife for death is but a dream and "sor-row still is life."
do not des-pair Up-on that day of free-dom yet will I be there.

THE PROLETARIAT

Key of F minor
Begins on C

Trans. from the Yiddish by
Evelyn Miller

"Un Du Ackerst"
Russian Bund Song about 1900

With marked Rhythm

1. You work with ham-mer and with axe Weave the wool and spin the flax. From the
2. You mine the ir-on and the tin, Sow the seed, then gath-er in, Bring to
3. You gath-er treas-ures for the few, Prec-ious jewels but none for you. And from
4. Man — of la-bor, but a-wake, With your strength these fet-ters break. If you

cho.

ma-ny spools you spin, Say, my peo-ple what you win.
ta-bles ves-sels fine, Full of food and rar-est wine. Cling, clang, cling, clang, Sings the
out your toil and pain See, you weld your-self a chain.
will it, they shall see Your mighty hands have set you free.

ham-mer his might-y song ; Cling, clang, cling, clang, Burst the chains and free the throng.

9

HEIRS OF TIME

Key of G
Begins on G

Thomas Wentworth Higginson

J. Naylor

Sturdily

1. From street and square, from hill and glen, Of this vast world be-yond my door, I
2. Not er-mine clad or clothed in state, Their ti-tle-deeds not yet made plain, But
3. The peas-ant brain shall yet be wise, The un-tamed pulse grow calm and still; The
4. Some day, with-out a trum-pet's call This news will o'er the world be blown: "The

hear the tread of march-ing men, The pa-tient ar-mies of the poor.
wak-ing ear-ly, toil-ing late, The heirs of all the earth re-main.
blind shall see, the low-ly rise, To work in peace Time's won-drous will.
her-i-tage comes back to all! The myr-iad mon-archs take their own."

Ancient Jewish Lullaby

Key of G minor
Begins on G

Words from Yiddish by M.E. Gallagher
Not too slowly, but with tenderness.

Traditional air
harmonized by Liebich

Sleep, my child, sleep, my dar-ling, All too soon my song will cease When you have left my arms so lov-ing,
'Tho life of-fers pain and sor-row To the hum-ble low-ly born, Yet there will be for all a bright to-mor-row.
Work and love your toil-ing broth-er While you sing a song of peace. When work-ers clasp hands with each oth-er,

May you then find a life of peace. When you have left my arms so lov-ing, May you then find a life of peace.
Work, my child, for that hap-py morn. Yet there will be for all a bright to-mor-row. Work, my child, for that hap-py morn.
Then the whole world will be at peace. When work-ers clasp hands with each oth-er, Then the whole world will be at peace.

HALLELUJAH, I'M A BUM

Key of F
Begins on C

"Revive Us Again"
Gospel Hymn

Harry McClintock

1. "Oh, why don't you work   Like— other men do?" "How the
2. "Oh, why don't you pray   For — your dail-y bread?" "If—
3. "Oh, why don't you save   All the mon-ey you earn?" "If—
4. I do love my boss,   He's a   good friend of mine. That's

hell can I   work When there's no work   to   do?"
that's all I   did, I'd   be might-y   soon   dead" Hal-le-
I did-n't   eat, I'd   have mon-ey   to   burn."
why I'm   starv-ing Out on the   bread   line.

lu—jah, I'm a   bum;   Hal-le—lu—jah bum a-

gain Ha-le-lu-jah, give us a hand-out to re-vive us a—gain.

SOLIDARITY FOREVER

Key of B
Begins on F
Ralph Chaplin

"Battle Hymn of the Republic"

1 When the Un—ion's in-spi-ra-tion thru the work-er's blood shall run, There can
2 It is we who plowed the prai-ries; built the cit—ies where they trade; Dug the
3 They have tak-en un—told mil-lions that they nev—er toiled to earn, But with-
4 In our hands is placed a pow-er great-er than their hoard-ed gold; Great-er

be no pow-er great-er an—y where beneath the sun. Yet what force on earth is weak-er than the
mines & built the work-shops; end-less miles of rail-road laid Now we stand out-cast and starv-ing 'mid the
out our brain and mus-cle not a sin-gle wheel can turn. We can break their haughty pow-er, gain our
than the might of arm-ies mag-ni-fied a thous-and fold We can bring to birth the new world from the

Chorus

fee-ble strength of one? But the Un—ion makes us strong.
won-ders we have made; But the Un—ion makes us strong.
free-dom when we learn That the Un—ion makes us strong.
ash-es of the old, For the Un—ion makes us strong

Sol— i-dar-i-ty for-

ev— er! Sol— i-dar-i-ty for- ev— er!

Sol— i-dar-i-ty for-ev— er! For the Un-ion makes us strong.

12

WORKERS OF THE WORLD, AWAKEN!

Key of G
Begins on D
Joe Hill

Joe Hill

Quickly

1. Work-ers of the world, a-wak-en ! Break your chains, de-mand your rights.
2. If the work-ers take a no-tion, They can stop all speed-ing trains;
3. Join the un-ion fel-low work-ers, Men and wom-en side by side;
4. Work-ers of the world, a-wak-en! Rise in all your splen-did might;

All the wealth you make is tak-en   By ex-ploit-ing par-a-sites.
Ev'-ry ship up-on the o-cean   They can tie with might-y chains;
We will crush the greed-y shirk-ers   Like a sweep-ing surg-ing tide:
Take the wealth that you are mak-ing, It be-longs to you by right.

Shall you kneel in deep sub-mis-sion   From your cra-dles to your graves?
Ev'-ry wheel in the cre-a-tion,   Ev'-ry mine and ev'-ry mill,
For u-nit-ed we are stand-ing,   But di-vid-ed we will fall:
No one will for bread be cry-ing,   We'll have free-dom, love and health,

Is the height of your am-bi-tion   To be good and will-ing slaves?
Fleets and arm-ies of the na-tion,   Will at their com-mand stand still.
Let this be our un-der-stand-ing--- "All for one and one for all."
When the grand red flag is fly-ing   In the work-ers' Com-mon-wealth.

SOUP SONG

Key of B♭
Begins on F

"My Bonnie Lies
Over the Ocean"

Maurice Sugar

1. I'm spend-ing my nights at the flop-house; I'm spend-ing my days on the street—
2. I spent twen-ty years in the fac-tory, I did ev'-ry-thing I was told—
3. I saved fif-teen bucks with my bank-er To buy me a car and a yacht—

—; I'm look-ing for work but I find none—; I wish I had some-thing to eat —
—. They said I was loy-al and faith-ful— But e-ven be-fore I get old—
—. I went down to draw out my for-tune — But this is the an-swer I got —

Soo-op, soo — op, They give me a bowl of soo-oo-op.

Soo — op , soo — op, They give me a bowl of soup———.

14

THE PREACHER AND THE SLAVE

Key of G
Begins on D
Joe Hill

"In the Sweet
Bye and Bye"
Gospel Hymn

1. Long-haired preachers come out ev'ry night, Try to tell you what's wrong & what's right; But when
2. If you fight hard for children and wife Try to get something good in this life, You're a
3. Work-ing-men of all countries, u-nite! Side by side we for freedom will fight; When the

asked how 'bout something to eat, They will an-swer with voices so sweet: } You will
sin-ner and bad man, they tell, When you die you will sure go to hell. } You will
world and its wealth we have gained, To the grafters we'll sing this re-frain: You will

chorus

eat   bye and bye   In that glor-i-ous land a-bove the sky;   Work and
eat   bye and bye   When you've learned how to cook and to — fry.   Chop some

pray,   live on hay,   You'll get pie in the sky when you die. (It's a lie)
wood, 'twill do you good,   And you'll eat in the sweet bye and bye.

I'M LABOR

Samuel H. Friedman

Harry Mayer

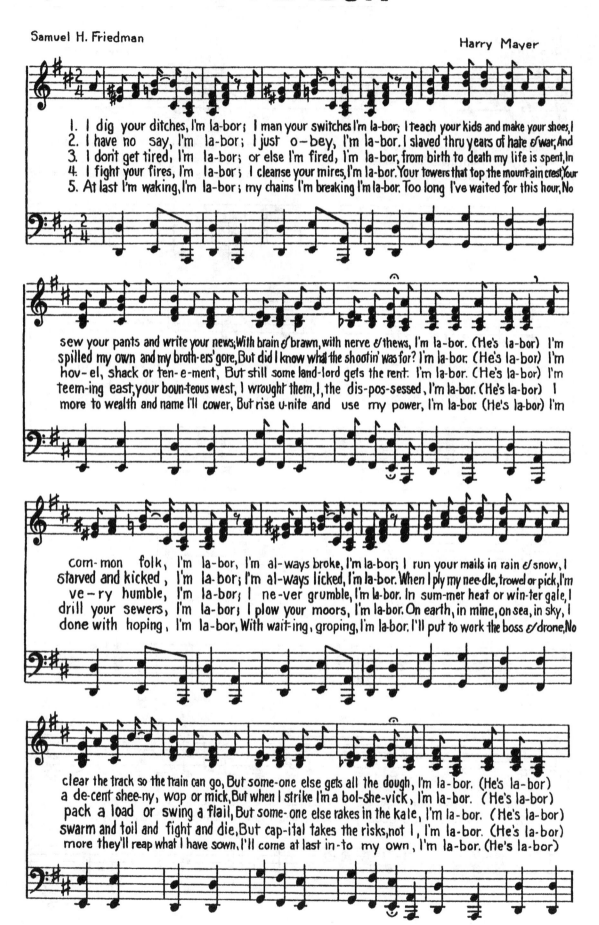

1. I dig your ditches, I'm la-bor; I man your switches I'm la-bor; I teach your kids and make your shoes, I
2. I have no say, I'm la-bor; I just o-bey, I'm la-bor. I slaved thru years of hate & war, And
3. I don't get tired, I'm la-bor; or else I'm fired, I'm la-bor, from birth to death my life is spent, In
4. I fight your fires, I'm la-bor; I cleanse your mires, I'm la-bor. Your towers that top the mount-ain crest, Your
5. At last I'm waking, I'm la-bor; my chains I'm breaking I'm la-bor. Too long I've waited for this hour, No

sew your pants and write your news; With brain & brawn, with nerve & thews, I'm la-bor. (He's la-bor) I'm
spilled my own and my broth-ers' gore, But did I know what the shootin' was for? I'm la-bor. (He's la-bor) I'm
hov-el, shack or ten-e-ment, But still some land-lord gets the rent. I'm la-bor. (He's la-bor) I'm
teem-ing east, your boun-teous west, I wrought them, I, the dis-pos-sessed, I'm la-bor. (He's la-bor) I
more to wealth and name I'll cower, But rise u-nite and use my power, I'm la-bor. (He's la-bor) I'm

com-mon folk, I'm la-bor, I'm al-ways broke, I'm la-bor; I run your mails in rain & snow, I
starved and kicked, I'm la-bor; I'm al-ways licked, I'm la-bor. When I ply my nee-dle, trowel or pick, I'm
ve-ry humble, I'm la-bor; I ne-ver grumble, I'm la-bor. In sum-mer heat or win-ter gale, I
drill your sewers, I'm la-bor; I plow your moors, I'm la-bor. On earth, in mine, on sea, in sky, I
done with hoping, I'm la-bor, With wait-ing, groping, I'm la-bor. I'll put to work the boss & drone, No

clear the track so the train can go, But some-one else gets all the dough, I'm la-bor. (He's la-bor)
a de-cent shee-ny, wop or mick, But when I strike I'm a bol-she-vick, I'm la-bor. (He's la-bor)
pack a load or swing a flail, But some-one else rakes in the kale, I'm la-bor. (He's la-bor)
swarm and toil and fight and die, But cap-ital takes the risks, not I, I'm la-bor. (He's la-bor)
more they'll reap what I have sown, I'll come at last in-to my own, I'm la-bor. (He's la-bor)

16

HOLD THE FORT

Music by Philip Bliss, 1870

Steady march time

1. We meet to-day in free-dom's cause And raise our voic-es high. We'll
2. — Look, my com-rades see the un-ion Ban-ners wav-ing high; —
3. — See our num-bers still in-creas-ing, Hear the bu-gles blow; —
4. — Fierce and long the bat-tle ra-ges, But we shall not fear. —

join our hands in un—ion strong To bat—tle or to die ———.
Re - in-force-ments now ap-pear-ing, Vic-to-ry is nigh ———.
By our un-ion we shall tri-umph O-ver ev-'ry foe ———.
Help will come when-e'er its need-ed Cheer, my com-rades, cheer——!

Refrain

Hold the fort for we are com-ing, Un—ion men be strong.

Side by side we bat-tle on-ward, Vic-to-ry will   come.

STEP, STEP

Key of F minor
Begins on C
Swedish Folk Song

Marching time

Step, step, keep the step, It is more than half your power. If in step you come by hun-dreds,

No one stops to look or won-der. If in step you come by thou-sands, May-be one will pause to

lend his ear. But with hundreds, thousands, millions, All will hear your marching thunder.

THESE THINGS SHALL BE

Key of G
Begins on D
John A. Symonds
"Truro"
Thomas Williams

1. These things shall be — a loft-ier race Than e'er the world hath known shall rise
2. They shall be gen-tle, brave and strong To spill no drop of blood, but dare
3. Na-tion with na-tion, land with land, In-armed shall live as com-rades free;
4. New arts shall bloom of loft-ier mould, And might-ier mu-sic thrill the skies,

With flame of free-dom in their souls, And light of knowl-edge in their eyes:
All that may plant man's lord-ship firm On earth and fire, and sea, and air.
In ev-ery heart and brain shall throb The pulse of one fra-ter-ni-ty.
And ev-ery life shall be a song, When all the earth is par-a-dise. A-men.

WORKMEN'S CIRCLE HYMN

Key of G
Begins on D
Translated from the Yiddish by Samuel H. Friedman

M. Posner

1. 'Mid the blaze of a world in com-mo—tion The light of true free-dom we sought: Here at
2. On the an-vil of strug-gle cre-a——ted, The ring is our ar—mor and shield. The
(Members of unions sing the following — The un-ion's our ar—mor and shield.)

home and far o-ver the o——cean To the forge of our vis-ion we brought The
branch-es are links that are ma—ted In mould-ing the wea-pon we wield So

fire of our love and de—vo—tion And our own work-men's Cir-cle we wrought.
(Members of unions sing —————And a un—ion of work-ers we wrought.)
for-ward with zeal un-a-ba—ted Our fer-vor will con-quer the field.

Cho.

A time-less bond u-nites us, A ring of tem-pered steel. One ra-diant bea-con lights us To

peace and com-mon weal. Stand all for one and one for all, The work-ing class i-deal.

19

BREAD and ROSES

Key of G
Begins on D

Arturo Giovannitti
Translated by S.H.F.

Giuseppe Adami

1. Shout the mes – sage to the breez – es, Far and wide & to each
2. On the march to gain our free – dom, We pro – claim the faith that's
3. Work-ers join us from all ra – ces, Ev – er hop-ing, marching

neigh – bor, Hail the voice & soul of La – bor, Hail our
in us. Faith and for-ti-tude will win us La – bor's
fight – ing, We've un-furled the flag u – nit-ing With us

Lo – cal eight-y nine ——.
fight for li – ber-ty ——. Ral-ly com – rades a-rise and
all hu man-i – ty ——.

for – ward, On the mor-row we shall see —— Bread and

ro – ses, song and laugh-ter, Won by sol-i-dar-i – ty ——.

BREAD and ROSES

Key of Ab
Begins on Ab
James Oppenheim

Caroline Kohlsaat

Steady march time

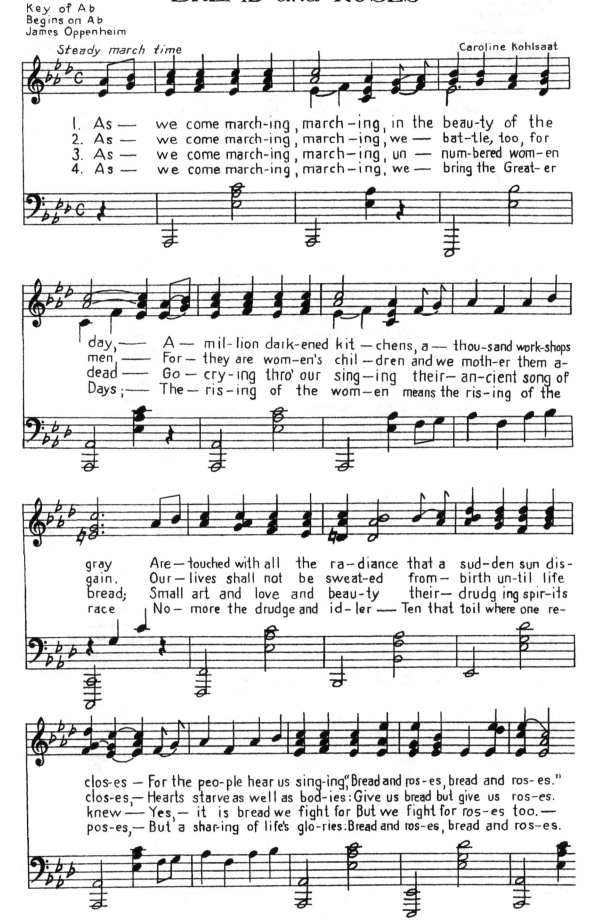

1. As — we come march-ing, march-ing, in the beau-ty of the day, — A — mil-lion dark-ened kit — chens, a — thou-sand work-shops gray Are — touched with all the ra-diance that a sud-den sun dis-clos-es — For the peo-ple hear us sing-ing "Bread and ros-es, bread and ros-es."

2. As — we come march-ing, march-ing, we — bat-tle, too, for men — For — they are wom-en's chil — dren and we moth-er them a-gain. Our — lives shall not be sweat-ed from — birth un-til life clos-es, — Hearts starve as well as bod-ies: Give us bread but give us ros-es.

3. As — we come march-ing, march-ing, un — num-bered wom-en dead — Go — cry-ing thro' our sing-ing their — an-cient song of bread; Small art and love and beau-ty their — drudg ing spir-its knew — Yes, — it is bread we fight for But we fight for ros-es too. —

4. As — we come march-ing, march-ing, we — bring the Great-er Days; — The — ris-ing of the wom-en means the ris-ing of the race No — more the drudge and id-ler — Ten that toil where one re-pos-es, — But a shar-ing of life's glo-ries: Bread and ros-es, bread and ros-es.

THE LAND OF THE NOONDAY NIGHT

key of B minor
Begins on F#
Ernest Howard Crosby

Eleanor Smith

Somewhat Slowly

1. We have eyes to see like you, In the heart of the deep, deep mine, But there's
2. But our home is not like yours; 'Tis a bare, un- paint-ed shack, Where the
3. And we la-bor with strain-ing arms For the pit-tance they deign to give, And our
4. Who was it made the coal? Our God as well as theirs! If he

nothing to mark but the dreadful dark, Where the sun can ne-ver shine. On
rain-drops pour on the shak-y floor, And the coal-dust stains it black. Not
boys must quit the school for the pit To drudge that we all may live. And
gave it free to you and to me, Then keep us out who dares! Let

the banks of clammy coal Our lamps cast a flick'ring light, At the
a flow'r or blade of grass Can es- cape the grim-y blight, For the
our teeth feel the grit of the mine In the very bread we bite, And our
the peo-ple have their mines, Their own by im-mort-al right, And good

bot-tom drear of the moist black hole In the land of the noon-day night.
face of our yard is seared and scarred In the land of the noon-day night.
in- most soul is de-filed with coal In the land of the noon-day night.
pre-vail un- der hill and dale In the land of the noon-day night.

Brothers, to Light and to Freedom

Key of Bb
Begins on F

Translated from the German

Russian Folk Song

1. Broth-ers to light and to free-dom   Broth-ers, a-wake to the day;
2. See how the mil-lions are grop-ing,   Seek-ing a-way thru the night.
3. Hun-ger and chains were our por-tion,   Feed-ing like beg-gars on crumbs.
4. Firm is our faith we shall con-quer,   Slav-er-y's yoke we shall break.

Break-ing with joy on the dark past   A fu-ture is light-ing the way!
Let us re-solve that we shall seek   Al-ways the free-ing light.
Now light is pierc-ing the dark-ness,   Dawn of de-liv-er-ance comes.
Wel-com-ing death e-ven gai-ly,   Fight-ing for lib-er-ty's sake.

Break-ing with joy on the dark past,   A fu-ture is light-ing the way!
Let us re-solve that we shall seek   Al-ways the free-ing light.
Now light is pierc-ing the dark-ness,   Dawn of de-liv-er-ance comes.
Wel-com-ing death e-ven gai-ly,   Fight-ing for lib-er-ty's sake.

23

BREAD

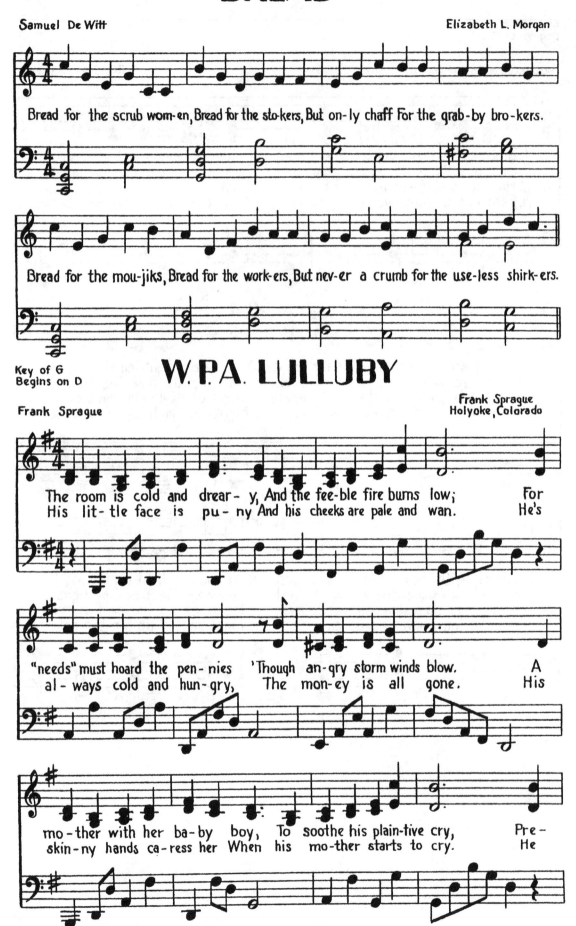

Key of C
Begins on C

Samuel De Witt

Elizabeth L. Morgan

Bread for the scrub wom-en, Bread for the sto-kers, But on-ly chaff For the grab-by bro-kers.

Bread for the mou-jiks, Bread for the work-ers, But nev-er a crumb for the use-less shirk-ers.

W. P. A. LULLUBY

Key of G
Begins on D

Frank Sprague

Frank Sprague
Holyoke, Colorado

The room is cold and drear-y, And the fee-ble fire burns low; For
His lit-tle face is pu-ny And his cheeks are pale and wan. He's

"needs" must hoard the pen-nies, 'Though an-gry storm winds blow. A
al-ways cold and hun-gry, The mon-ey is all gone. His

mo-ther with her ba-by boy, To soothe his plain-tive cry, Pre-
skin-ny hands ca-ress her When his mo-ther starts to cry. He

tends that they are hap-py,   And sings this lul - la - by :
says,"Let's play at make believe And sing our lul - la - by."

W. P. A.   for pa - pa And a pen-sion for gran-dad. —

You   may be   the Pres - i - dent;   Gee but ma-ma's   glad.

Swing   him high and swing him low,   Won'l that be   just grand

When they shout my ba-by's name And play   the big   brass   band.

ANTHEM OF THE INTERNATIONAL LADIES GARMENT WORKERS' UNION

Key of G, Begins on D
Emily B. Fine

Luigi Papavello

With Spirit

1. One bat-tle is won But the fight's just be-gun And the un-ion flag's un-
South, East, and West, All the work-ers op-pressed Join the un-ion rank's to-

furled———: U — ni-ted we're strong Let us march toward the dawn Of a
day———; Our ban-ners are bright As they float red and white Where our

chorus

brave new work-ers world—. Oh, Un-ion of the Gar-ment Work-ers, To
Union leads the way—.

you we ev-er will be true———. We'll build and we'll fight And we'll

rise in our might With the I. L. G. W. U——. 2. North, U——.

26

BANDIERA ROSSA
The Scarlet Banner

Translation by Samuel H. Friedman

Italian Worker's Song

Lively march time

Avanti popolo, a la rescossa, Bandiera rossa, bandiera rossa.
1. A-rise, O Com-rades, and take your sta-tion, Be-hind our ban-ner, The Scar-let ban-ner!
2. From field and work-shop and mine ap-pear-ing Be-hind our ban-ner, The Scar-let ban-ner!
3. One fear-less work-er and then an-oth-er Be-hind our ban-ner, The Scar-let ban-ner!

Avanti popolo, a la rescossa, Bandiera rossa trionferà.
To-geth-er win our e-man-ci-pa-tion, In ev'-ry na-tion tri-um-phant-ly.
On land and wa-ter our call they're hear-ing, The hour is near-ing tri-um-phant-ly.
Have lit a fire no re-pulse can smoth-er, Stand up, my broth-er tri-um-phant-ly.

Cho.

Bandiera rossa trionferà, Bandiera rossa trionferà,
Up, Scar-let Ban-ner, and front the foe; Up Scar-let Ban-ner and for-ward go!

Bandiera rossa trionferà Evivva socialisma e la liberta.
Up, Scar-let Ban-ner, that the world may see So-cial-is-m tri-umph-ing and li-ber-ty.

The March of the Hungry Men

Key of C Minor
Begins on Eb

Reginald Wright Kaufman

Agnes Cunningham

Steady march time

1. In the dreams of your down-y couch-es, Thru the shades of your pam-pered sleep, Give
2. So comes an-oth-er arm-y, Your wit can-not com-pute, The
3. And some come emp-ty hand-ed, With fin-gers gnarled and strong, And
4. Thru the depths of the Dev-ils dark-ness, With the dis-tant stars for light, They are

ear, you can hear it com-ing, The tide that is stead-y and deep—Give ear for the sound is
man at arms self fash-ioned, The man you made the brute, From the farm and sweat-shop
some come dumb with sor-row, And some come drunk with song; But all that you thot were
com-ing, the while you slum-ber, And they come with the might of Right. On a mor-row per-haps to-

grow-ing, From des-ert & dun-geon & den; The tramp of the hun-gry mil-lions, The
gath-ered, From fac-to-ry, mine and mill, With lyre and shears and au-gur, Dib-
bur-ied Are stir-ring & lithe and quick. And they car-ry a brass bound scep-ter: The
mor-row--You will wa-ken & see, and then You will hand the keys of the cit-ies, To the

Refrain: *p   cresc. poco a poco*

march of the Hun-gry Men.
ble and drift and drill.   } Give ear for the sound is grow-ing From des-ert & dun-geon &
brass com-pos-ing stick.
ranks of the Hun-gry Men.

ff

den;   The tramp of the hun-gry mil-lions, The march of the Hun-gry Men.

28

The Little Red Hen Song

Kate B. Stockton

Gaily, but not too fast

Elizabeth Morgan

"Come be jolly, jolly, jolly, For it's folly, folly, folly, And only makes life harder to complain: The world is full of beauty, and co-ops lighten du – ty, Like sunshine, weaving rainbows in the rain. Brek-akeck-keck, Co-ops, Co-ops! Brek-akeck-keck, Co-ops, We'll sing and we'll dance, with hippety-hops. Hur-rah for Co-op-er – a – tion!"

The Farmer's and Worker's Song

Key of A
Begins on A

"The Bulldog on the Bank"

1. Oh, the farm-ers have no banks, And the bank-ers have a pool. Oh, the bank-ers own the
2. Said the work-ers to the courts, "We want to see fair play. Grant us our nat-ural
3. Oh, the "sys-tem" stands for "class" And a-gainst the mass-es rule Not the heav-y el-e-

banks, and "No quar-ter is their rule. Said the farm-er to the bank-er "I'd like to use your
right And a 'liv-ing wage' as pay." Said the courts un-to the work-ers, "You'd bet-ter chase a-
phant, Nor the dem-o-crat-ic mule Will help the peo-ple out, So they bet-ter go to

pool." Said the bank-er to the farm-er, "Do you take me for a fool?"
way-- An-oth-er stiff in-junc-tion, Will suit your case to-day." Sing-ing tra la
school, Cre-ate their own new part-y, And quit be-ing Wall Street's tool!

la la la la la, Sing-ing tra la la la la la la, Sing-ing tra la la la la
la la
la la

la, Sing-ing tra la la la la la, Tra la la la, tra la la la, tra la la la la la.

30

WE HAVE FED YOU ALL

Key of C minor
Begins on G
"By an Unknown Proletarian"

Rudolf Liebich

1. We have fed you all for a thou-sand years And you hail us still un-
2. There is nev-er a mine blown sky-ward now But we're bur-ied a-live for

fed. Tho there's ne-ver a dol-lar of all your wealth But marks the work-ers dead. We have
you. There is ne-ver a wreck drifts shore-ward now But we are its ghast-ly crew. Go,

yield-ed our best to give you rest And you lie on a crim-son wool. Then if
reck-on our dead by the for-ges red And the fac-to-ries where we spin. If

blood be the price of all your wealth, Good God, we have paid it in full.
blood be the price of your curs-ed wealth, Good God, we have paid it in!

WE HAVE FED YOU ALL

3. We have fed you all for a thou-sand years. For that was our doom you know, From the day when you chained us in your fields To the strike of a week a-go. You have eat-en our lives and our ba-bies and wives And we're told it's your le-gal share. But if blood be the price of your law-ful wealth, Good God! we have bought it fair!

Key of G minor
Begins on G

ONWARD BROTHERS

"Ebenezer"
(Ton y Botel)

Llawlyfr Moliant, 1890
Arr'd. by T. J. Williams

Havelock Ellis

With dignity

1. On-ward Broth-ers, march still on-ward Side by side to car-ry on.
2. Old-en sag-es saw it dim-ly, And their joy to rap-ture wrought;
3. Still strong deeds and brave are need-ed, Still the toil for free-dom's cause.

Though the night be dark and hope-less, We are com-ing toward the Dawn.
Liv-ing men have gazed up-on it, Stand-ing on the hills of thought.
Let us all join in to-geth-er, Fight a-gainst the mas-ter's laws.

Wom-en, chil-dren, slave a-bout us, Hard the toil and grim the strife.
All the past has done and suf-fered, All the dar-ing and the strife,
Let us strive for love and jus-tice, Broth-er-hood--true Free-dom's sun.

But our souls still sing with-in us, Dream-ing of a bet-ter life.
All has helped to mold the fu-ture, Make man mas-ter of his life.
Let us nev-er yield or fal-ter Till the vic-to-ry is won.

THE PEAT BOG SOLDIERS

Key of E minor
Begins on E
In march rhythm

Music by Rudi Goguel

Johann Esser and Wolfgang Langhoff

1. Far and wide as the eye can wan-der Heath and
2. Up and down the guards are pac-ing, No one,
3. But for us there is no com-plain-ing, Win-ter

bog are ev-ry where. Not a bird sings
no one can go through. Flight would mean a
will in time be past; One day we shall

out to cheer us Oaks are stand-ing gaunt and bare
sure death fac-ing, Guns and barbed wire greet our view.
cry re-joic-ing, "Home-land dear, you're mine at last."

Chorus

1&2 We are the peat-bog sol — diers; We're march-ing
3 Then will the peat-bog sol — diers March no more

with our spades To the bog. —
with their spades To the bog. —

COOPERATION IS OUR AIM

Key of C
Begins on G

"There Is a Tavern in the Town"

1. Co-op-er-a-tion is our aim, is our aim, We know thru that we'll sure-ly gain, surely gain Our
2. Come chil-dren all, we need you, too, need you too. There's plenty o' work for you to do, you to do. Let's
3. We'll build a house both wide and deep, wide and deep, With plenty o' room for hands & feet, hands & feet; With

due as men who till the fer-tile soil, And feed the hun-gry of the land, of the land
start right in, to-geth-er we can win, So all to-geth-er let's be-gin, let's be-gin. {Come on,
food and clothes and fun   for all, Thru win-ter, sum-mer, spring & fall, spring & fall}

far-mers, don't you tar-ry for we need Tom, Dick & Har-ry, We can make the grade if on-ly you'll co-

op-er-ate. Co-op-er-a-tion is our aim, is our aim. We know thru that we'll sure-ly

gain, sure-ly gain, Our   due as men who till the fer-tile soil, And feed the hun-gry of the land.

COME, RALLY YOUTH

Key of D minor
Begins on D
Samuel H. Friedman

German Folk Song
Arranged by
Dorothy Bachman

1. Come ral-ly youth of ev'ry na-tion, Swing axe, and cleave! We're
2. All hearts a-throb with stern e-la-tion, Thrust, spade, and heave! We're
3. Stone mates with iron in ex-ul-ta-tion, Lift, sledge, and swing! We're
4. Great tow-ers rise in con-se-cra-tion, Pierce, riv-ets cling! We're

clear-ing ground for the new foun-da-tion, Swing, axe, and cleave!
dig-ging deep for the new foun-da-tion, Thrust, spade and heave!
build-ing strong on the new foun-da-tion, Lift, sledge and swing!
soar-ing high from the new foun-da-tion, Pierce, riv-ets cling!

Youth, be bold, Scrap the old, Bat-ter down the walls where truth is sold.

Youth, be true, Build the new, Build-ers of the fu-ture world are you!

THE OATH
(Die Shruoh)

Key of D minor
Begins on D

Trans. from the Yiddish
by Samuel H. Friedman

Folk Song of the Bundist
Revolution in Russia, 1905

1. Broth-ers and sis-ters who've starved and bled, Har-ried and scat-tered o-ver all the world, Come gath-er to-geth-er, our flag is un-furled, The flag of wrath our blood has dyed—the ban-ner of red. Come swear we'll bear it on-ward,

2. We swear we will bat-tle for free-dom and right, As-sail the op-pres-sor and tram-ple his tools; We swear we will con-quer the dark-ness that rules, And storm the gate of tyr-an-ny or fall in the fight. Come swear we'll bear it on-ward,

3. We swear we'll not flinch in our ho-ly cru-sade As long as op-pres-sion and hun-ger en-dure; No more slave and mas-ter, no more rich and poor, A fel-low-ship of free men in a world we've re-made. We swear we'll bear it on-ward,

Cho.
liv-ing and dead! Heav'n and earth will bear wit-ness for us, Stars hear our fer-vent cho-rus,

The pledge of blood and tears we share. We swear, we swear, we — swear.

37

AIN'T GONNA STUDY WAR NO MORE

Key of F
Begins on F

Old Spiritual

Deliberately

1. Gon-na lay down my bur-den Down by the riv-er-side, Down by the riv-er-side,
2. Gon-na lay down my sword and shield Down by the riv-er-side Down by the riv-er-side,
3. Gon-na ride with my Prince of Peace Down by the riv-er-side Down by the riv-er-side,

Down by the riv-er-side, Gon-na lay down my bur-den Down by the riv-er-side. Ain't gon-na
Down by the riv-er-side. Gon-na lay down my sword and shield Down by the riv-er-side. Ain't gon-na
Down by the riv-er-side. Gon-na ride with my Prince of Peace. Down by the riv-er-side. Ain't gon-na

Cho.

stud-y war no more.
stud-y war no more.
stud-y war no more.

Ain't gon-na stud-y war no more. Ain't gon-na

stud-y war no more. Ain't gon-na stud-y war no more. Ain't gon-na

stud-y war no more. Ain't gon-na stud-y war no more. Ain't gon-na stud-y war no more.

HAIL THE HERO WORKERS

Key of Ab
Begins on C
Anna Garlin Spencer, 1851

Rosmore.
Henry G. Trembath, 1893

Hail the he-ro work-ers Of the might-y past! They whose la-bor build- ed
Hail ye, he-ro work-ers, Who to-day do hear Du-ty's myr-iad voic-es,
Hail ye, he-ro work-ers, Ye who yet shall come, When to this world's call-ing

All the things that last; Tho'ts of wis-est mean-ing, Deed's of no-blest right,
Sound-ing high and clear; Ye who quick re-spond-ing, Haste ye to your task,
All our lips are dumb. Ye shall build more no-bly, If our work be true,

Pa-tient toil in weak-ness, Struggles in the night; Hail, then, no-ble work-ers,
Be it grand or sim-ple, Ye for-get to ask ; Hail, ye, no-ble work-ers,
As we pass life's treas-ure On from old to new. Hail, ye, then, all work-ers,

Build-ers of the past, All whose lives have blest us With the gains that last.
Build-ers of to-day, Who life's treas-ure gath-er, that shall last al — way.
Of all lands and time, One brave band of he-roes, With one task sub-lime. A-men.

THE FARMER COMES TO TOWN

Key of F
Begins on A

American Folk Tune

When the farm-er comes to town With his wag-on brok-en down, O, the farm-er is the man who feeds them
When the law-yer hangs a-round, While the butcher cuts a pound, O, the farm-er is the man who feeds them
When the bank-er says he's broke, And the merchant's up in smoke, They for-get that it's the farm-er feeds them

all.   If you'll on-ly look and see, I think you will a-gree That the farm-er is the man who feeds them
all.   And the preach-er & the cook, Go a-stroll-ing by the brook, O, the farm-er is the man who feeds them
all.   It would put them to a test If the farm-er takes a rest—Then they'd know that it's the farm-er feeds them

all.   The farm-er is the man, The farm-er is the man, Lives on cred-it 'til the fall; Then they
all.   The farm-er is the man, The farm-er is the man, Lives on cred-it 'til the fall. With the
all.   The farm-er is the man, The farm-er is the man, Lives on cred-it 'til the fall;   And his

take him by the hand & they lead him from the land & the mid-dle man's the one who gets it all.
in-terest rate so high It's a won-der he don't die, for the mort-gage man's the one who gets it all.
pants are wear-ing thin, His con-di-tion it's a sin; He's for-got that he's the man who feeds them all.

COME, COMRADES, COME!

Key of C minor
Begins on G

William Morris

"Down Among the Dead Men"
Old drinking song

1. Come, com-rades, come, your glass—es clink; Up with your hands a health to drink--- The health of all that work—ers be, In ev'—ry land, on ev'—ry sea.

2. Well done! Now drink an-oth—er toast, And pledge the gath—'ring of the host---- The peo—ple, armed in brain and hand, To claim their rights in ev'—ry land.

3. Now, com—rades, let the glass blush red; Drink we the un—for—got—ten dead That did their deeds and went a—way Be—fore the bright sun brought the day.

4. The day? Ah, friends, late grows the night; Drink to the glim—mering spark of light, The her—ald of the joy to be, The bat—tle—torch of thee and me!

And he that will this health de—ny, Down a—mong the dead men, down a—mong the dead men,

Down, down, down, down, Down a—mong the dead men let him lie!

slower

HOLIDAY MARCH

Key of B♭
Begins on D

Frank Sprague   Frank Sprague

1. There are twen-ty mil-lion work-ers in the dear old U. S. A. Who can find no use-ful work that they can
2. There are twen-ty mil-lion farm-ers in the dear old U. S. A. Who will each one lose his lit-tle farm &

do.   They are home-less & half starv-ing And their lives are fil led with woe. There are
home.   Then the rich who own the na-tion Can a-muse them-selves each day Watch-ing

twen-ty mil-lion starv-ing chil-dren, too.   There's a bunch of crooks & law-yers In our
for-ty mil-lion hun-gry work-ers roam.   But be sure and don't get rad-i-cal; Keep

leg-is-la-tive halls Who make laws to rob the com-mon man who toils. They o-bey their mon-ey
both feet on the ground; An un-just law is sa-cred we are told.   So bow down your head in

mas-ters, Do what they are told to do, And pro-tect their rob ber mas-ters With their spoils.
sor- row, Be an ab-ject cring-ing slave, Let your wife & ba-bies Starve out in the cold.

No place to go; no work to do; Starv-ing where food a-bounds.

No fires to warm through bit-ter storms; No hopes but just dirt mounds.

WORKERS TOGETHER

Key of G
Begins on D

John Irwin, 1932

Grades 5B, 5A. McKinley School
Gloversville, N.Y., 1932

1. O, God, Thy rain and sun and soil Are joined with hu-man toil. To
2. We thank our God for sun and soil, Our broth-er man for toil. A-

bring from ev'-ry clime and land These boun-ties to our hand.
part from all not one could live, And so our thanks we give.

THE INTERNATIONALE

Key of A
Begins on E

Original French by Eugene Pottier

Translation by Charles H. Kerr

Pierre Degeyter

1. A-rise, ye pris'ners of star-va-tion! A-rise, ye wretch-ed of the earth! For
2. We want no con-des-cend-ing sa-viors To rule us from a judg-ment hall; We
3. Be-hold them seat-ed in their glo-ry, The kings of mine and rail and soil! What
4. Come all from shops and field u-nit-ed, The un-ion we of all who work, The

jus-tice thun-ders con-dem—na-tion, A bet-ter world's in birth. No
work-ers ask not for their fa-vors, Let us con-sult for all. To
have you read in all their sto-ry, But how they plun-dered toil? Fruits
earth be-longs to us, the work-ers, No room here for the shirk. How

more tra-di-tion's chains shall bind us A-rise ye slave no more in thrall. The
make the thief dis-gorge his boot-y, To free the spir-it from its cell, We
of the work-ers' toil are bur-ied In the strong cof-fers of a few; In
ma-ny on our flesh have fat-tened! But if the noi-some birds of prey Shall

44

earth shall rise on new foun-da-tions, We have been naught, we shall be all.

must our-selves de-cide our du-ty, We must de-cide and do it well.

work-ing for their res-ti-tu-tion The men will on-ly ask their due.

van-ish from the sky some morn-ing, The bless-ed sun-light still will stay.

Cho.

'Tis the fi-nal con-flict, Let each stand in his place, The

In-ter-na-tion-a-le Shall be the hu-man race. 'Tis the

fi-nal con-flict, Let each stand in his place, The

In-ter-na-tion-a———le Shall be the hu-man race.

45

I've Heard the Workers Sing

Key of D minor
Begins on A

Yona Finkelstein

Russian folk tune

1. I've heard the work-ers sing And oh, the joy they bring! I've heard the cho-rus ring
2. They sing of roar-ing steam. They sing of Boss Ma-chine. They sing with bod-ies lean

— Be-neath the sun. What if they're tired and worn? What if their clothes are torn ? An-oth-er
—And hun-gry eyes, Of days when toil will end, Of days when man is friend, Days when the

song is born When day is done. They sing of fields of grain, Toil-ing in
songs will blend In joy-ous cries. To-mor-row's songs they sing-And oh, the

sun and rain. What if the back has pain ? They still can dream Of grain that will be bread,
joy they bring. I've heard their voi-ces ring In ev'ry clime. I know no songs so sweet-

— Of bodies that are fed , A roof a-bove the head, And time to dream.
—With-in my heart they beat, The sound of work-ers feet March-ing thru Time.

THE OLD CHISELLER

Key of F minor
Begins on C

Mark Starr

William Wolff

Deliberately

There was an old chis'-ler and his shop was a dump. The I. L. G. got after him. He did-n't know where to jump. He dodged and he twist-ed and he tried to run a—way. The Un-ion fol-lowed af-ter. Now fair wa-ges he must pay.

RIDE A FAST HORSE

Key of C

Begins on G

Samuel A. DeWitt

Elizabeth L. Morgan

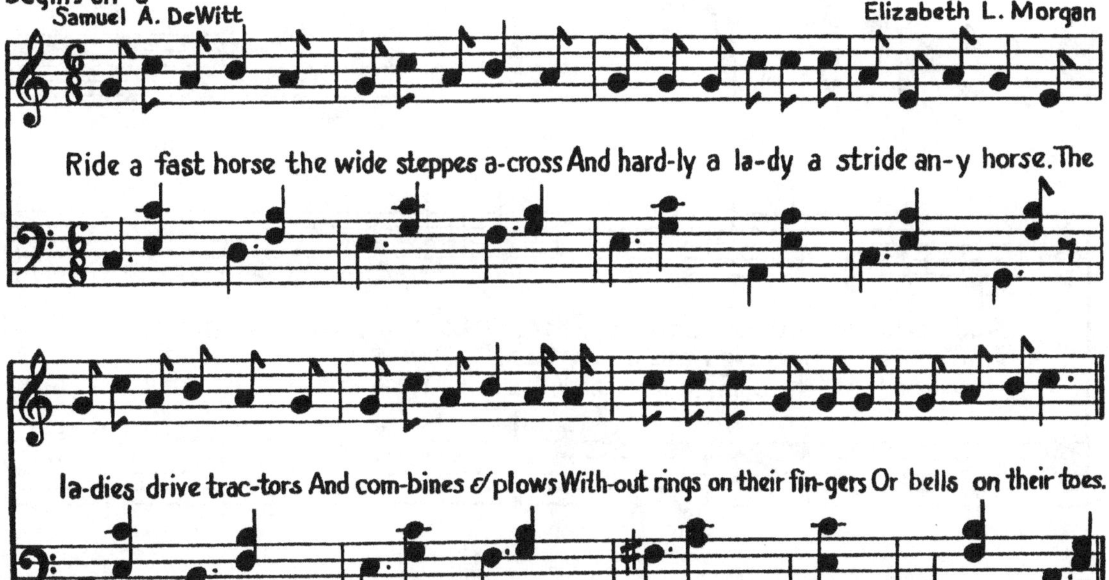

Ride a fast horse the wide steppes a-cross And hard-ly a la-dy a stride an-y horse. The la-dies drive trac-tors And com-bines & plows With-out rings on their fin-gers Or bells on their toes.

Not In Dumb Resignation

Key of G Minor
Begins on D

John Hay, 1891

"Llangloffan"
Welsh hymn tune from 1865

1. Not in dumb res-ig - na - tion We lift our hands on high;
2. When ty-rant feet are tramp-ling Up-on the com-mon weal,
3. Thy will! It strength-ens weak-ness, It bids the strong be just;

Not like the nerve-less fa-tal-ist Con-tent to trust and die:
Thou dost not bid us bend and writhe Be-neath the i - ron heel.
No lip to fawn, no hand to beg, No brow to seek the dust.

Our faith springs like the ea - gle, Who soars to meet the sun,
In Thy name we as - sert our right By sword and tongue or pen,
Wher - ev - er man op-press-es man Be - neath Thy lib - eral sun,

And cries ex-ult-ing un- to Thee, O Lord, Thy will be done!
And oft a peo-ple's wrath may flash Thy mes-sage un-to men.
O Lord, be there, Thine arm made bare, Thy right-eous will be done! A-men.

NO MORE MOURNING

Key of F
Begins on F

John Handcox

Oh Freedom

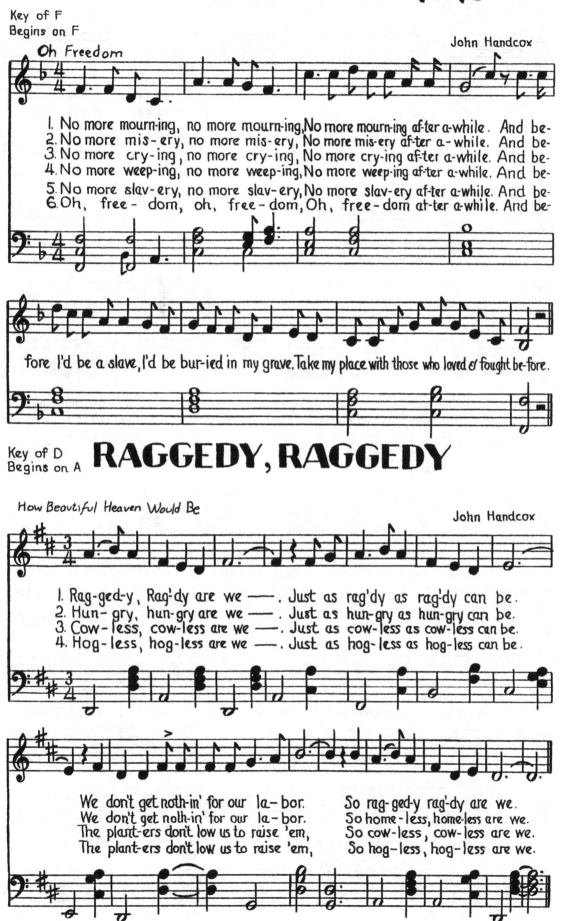

1. No more mourn-ing, no more mourn-ing, No more mourn-ing af-ter a-while. And be-
2. No more mis-ery, no more mis-ery, No more mis-ery af-ter a-while. And be-
3. No more cry-ing, no more cry-ing, No more cry-ing af-ter a-while. And be-
4. No more weep-ing, no more weep-ing, No more weep-ing af-ter a-while. And be-
5. No more slav-ery, no more slav-ery, No more slav-ery af-ter a-while. And be-
6. Oh, free-dom, oh, free-dom, Oh, free-dom at-ter a-while. And be-

fore I'd be a slave, I'd be bur-ied in my grave. Take my place with those who loved & fought be-fore.

RAGGEDY, RAGGEDY

Key of D
Begins on A

John Handcox

How Beautiful Heaven Would Be

1. Rag-ged-y, Rag'dy are we ——. Just as rag'dy as rag'dy can be.
2. Hun-gry, hun-gry are we ——. Just as hun-gry as hun-gry can be.
3. Cow-less, cow-less are we ——. Just as cow-less as cow-less can be.
4. Hog-less, hog-less are we ——. Just as hog-less as hog-less can be.

We don't get noth-in' for our la—bor.   So rag-ged-y rag'dy are we.
We don't get noth-in' for our la—bor.   So home-less, home-less are we.
The plant-ers don't low us to raise 'em,   So cow-less, cow-less are we.
The plant-ers don't low us to raise 'em,   So hog-less, hog-less are we.

49

TEN LITTLE SWEATSHOPS

Key of D
Begins on D
Moderato

William Wolff

Ten little sweatshops the bosses thought were fine, The union organized one—then there were nine!
Six little sweatshops, the union made a drive And picket-ed an-oth-er—then there were five!

Nine little sweatshops working very late, An-other bunch of workers struck—then there were eight!
Five little sweatshops rotten to the core, An-other sign-d up with the union—then there were four!

Eight little sweatshops stinking to high heaven, the sanitary code got one—then there were seven!
Four little sweatshops, they're going fast you see, One sold out to an-oth-er — then there were three!

Seven little sweatshops, you should hear the kicks the workers made about their pay—then there were six!
Three little sweatshops, the workers vowed to sue for back wages due to them—then there were two!

Two little sweatshops, an-other battle won By union sol-i-dar-i-ty—then there was one!

One lonely sweatshop our tale is almost done — All of them were organized. Now there are none!

ON THE PICKET LINE

Key of F
Begins on F

"Polly-Wolly-Doodle"

In a lively march time

1. To win our strike and all our de-mands Come & pick-et on the pick-et
2. If you've nev-er spent a night in jail Come and pick-et on the pick-et
3. If you don't like scabs and thugs & stools Come and pick-et on the pick-et

line. In one strong un-ion we'll join our hands, Come & pick-et on the pick-et
line; You will be in-vi-ted with-out fail; Come and pick-et on the pick-et
line; For you show your boss that the work-er rules When you pick-et on the pick-et

line. On the line, on the line, On the pick-el, pick-et

line, We'll shout & yell & fight like hell, On the pick-et, pick-et line.

THE ADVANCING PROLETAIRE

Key of C
Begins on C
Douglas

Rudolf Liebich

Sturdily – not too fast

1. We are com——ing all u-nit——ed, Throbbing with un-measured
2. Years of la——bor, years of an——guish, Gallows grim and dungeon

pow'r. Through the dark——ness un-affrighted We have wait——ed for this
cell, All your boast——ed pow'rs to vanquish Have but taught us to re-

hour. Now we rise be-fore us sweeping All the gall——ing ties that
bel; Now the might—y giant has risen From the slum——ber of the

bind, And our fie——ry veins are leaping With the blood of all mankind.
years, And for him your strongest prison Has no ter-rors and no fears.

chorus

We are coming un-for-giv——ing And the earth re-sounds our tread.

Bone and sinew of the liv——ing, Spir-it of the rebel dead.

You who sow'd the winds of sor-row Now the whirl—wind you must dare.

As you face upon the mor——row The Ad-vancing Pro-le—taire!

WHIRLWINDS OF DANGER

Key of D minor
Begins on A
Douglas Robson

Russian-Polish Folk Song
Arr. by Dorothy Bachman

1 Whirl-winds of dan-ger are rag-ing a-round us, O'er-whelm-ing forc-es of
2 Wom-en and chil-dren in hun-ger are call-ing. Shall we be si-lent to their
3 Off with the crown of the ty-rants of fa-vor! Down in the dust with the

dark-ness as-sail. Still in the fight see ad-vanc-ing be-fore us Red flag of lib-er-ty that
sor-row and woe, While in the fight see our broth-ers are fall-ing? Up then u-nit-ed and
prince and the peer! Strike off your chains, all ye brave sons of la-bor, Wake all hu-man-i-ty for

Chorus

yet shall pre-vail. Then for-ward, ye work-ers, free-dom a-waits you,
con-quer the foe!
vic-tory is near.

O'er all the world on the land and the sea. On with the fight for the

cause of hu-man-i-ty, March, march, ye toil-ers and the world shall be free!

A REBEL SONG

Key of G
Begins on D

James Connolly

Crawford-Morgan

With Spirit

1. Come work-ers sing a reb-el song A song of love and hate, Of love un-to the
2. We sing no more of wail-ing And no songs of sighs or tears; High are our hopes and
3. Out of the depths of mis-er-y We march with hearts of flame With wrath a-gainst the

low–ly And ha-tred to the false-ly great The great who trod our fath-ers down Who steal our children's
stout our hearts And ban-ished all our fears Our flag is raised a-bove us So that all the world may
ru–lers false Who wreck our man-hood's name The serf who licks the ty-rant's rod May bend for-giv-ing

Cho.

bread, Whose band of greed is stretched to rob The liv–ing and the dead.
see 'Tis la-bor's faith and la-bor's arm A-lone can la-bor free.
knee The slave who breaks his slav'-ry's chain A wrath-ful man must be.

They sing our reb-el

song as we proud-ly sweep a-long To end the age long tyr-ran-ny that makes for human tears. Our

march is near-er done with each set-ting of the sun And the tyrants might is pass-ing with the pass-ing of the years.

THE RED FLAG

Key of G
Begins on D

James Connell

"Maryland, My Maryland"

1. The peo-ple's flag is deep-est red; It shroud-ed oft our mar-tyred dead; And
2. Look round the French-man loves its blaze, The stur-dy Ger-man chants its praise; In
3. It well re-calls the tri-umphs past; It gives the hope of peace at last, The
4. It suits to-day the weak and base Whose thots are fixed on self and place To
5. It waved a-bove our in-fant might When all a-head seemed dark as night. It
6. With heads un-cov-ered swear we all To bear it on-ward till we fall. Come

Cho.

e'er their limbs were stiff and cold, Their heart's blood dyed its ev-'ry fold.
Mos-cow's halls its hymns are sung, Chi-ca- go swells the surg-ing throng.
ban-ner bright, the sym-bol plain, Of hu-man right, of hu-man gain.
cringe be-neath the rich-man's frown, And tear the sa-cred em-blem down.
wit-nessed ma-ny a deed and vow. We will not change its col-or now.
dun-geons dark or gal-lows grim, This song shall be our part-ing hymn.

Then

raise the scar-let stan-dard high! With-in its shade we'll live and die; Tho

cow-ards flinch and trai-tors sneer, We'll keep the red flag fly-ing here.

UNITED FRONT SONG

Key of F minor
Begins on C

Original German words
by Bert Brecht

Hanns Eisler

1. And just be-cause he's hu-man   A man would like a lit-tle bite to
2. And just be-cause he's hu-man   He does-n't like a pis-tol to his
3. And just be-cause he's a work-er The job is all his

eat.   He won't get full on a lot of talk That won't give him bread and meat.
head,   He wants no ser-vants un-der him And no boss o-ver his head.
own,   The lib-era-tion of the work-ing class Is the job of the work-ers a-lone.

Refrain

So, left, two, three, So, left, two, three, To the work that we must do, March

on in the work-ers' u-nit-ed front For you are a work-er too.

57

THE REVOLUTION

Key of D
Begins on F#
Arturo Giovannitti

Herman Epstein

A-rise, then! A-rise, then, Ye men of the plow and the ham-mer, Ye

men of the helm and the le-ver; And send forth to the four winds of the earth, And send

forth to the four winds of the earth Your new proc-la-ma-tion of free-dom, Of

free-dom, of free-dom, Which shall be the last, Which shall be — the last And shall a-bide for-ev-er more.

Through you, through your u-nit-ed strength, Or-der shall be-come e-qui-ty,

Law shall be-come lib-er-ty, Du-ty shall be-come love, And re-li-gion shall be-come

truth. Thru you, thru you the man beast shall die; And the man, the man be born. And

lo and be-hold, my broth-ers, Peace shall reign for-ev - er! And this shall be called the rev-o-

lu-tion. A-rise then! A-rise then. Ye men of the plow and the ham-mer, Ye

men of the helm and the le-ver And send forth to the four winds of the earth, And send

forth to the four winds of the earth Your new proc-la-ma-tion of free-dom, Of free-dom, Of

free-dom, Which shall be the last, Which shall be ~ the last and shall a-bide for-ev-er more.

THE YOUNG GUARDS

"Zu Mantua"
German Folk Song

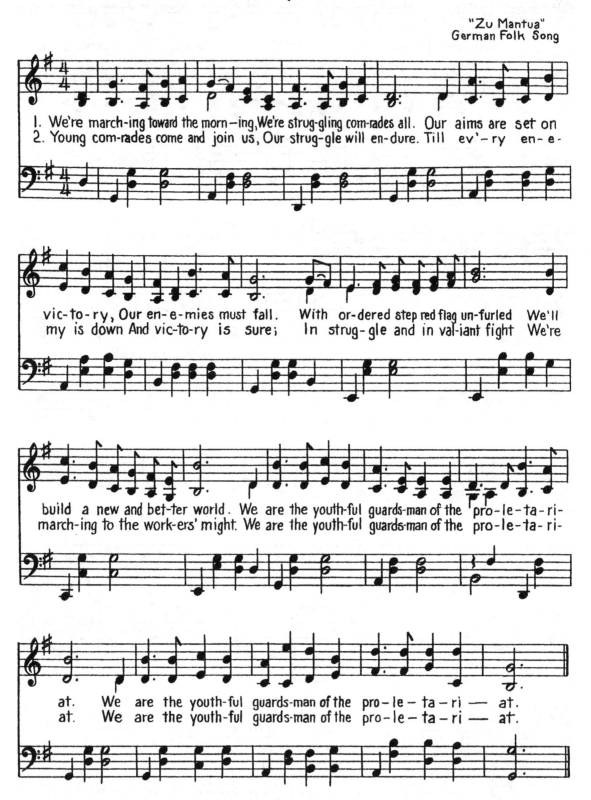

1. We're march-ing toward the morn-ing, We're strug-gling com-rades all. Our aims are set on
2. Young com-rades come and join us, Our strug-gle will en-dure. Till ev'-ry en-e-

vic-to-ry, Our en-e-mies must fall. With or-dered step red flag un-furled We'll
my is down And vic-to-ry is sure; In strug-gle and in val-iant fight We're

build a new and bet-ter world. We are the youth-ful guards-man of the pro-le-ta-ri-
march-ing to the work-ers' might. We are the youth-ful guards-man of the pro-le-ta-ri-

at. We are the youth-ful guards-man of the pro-le-ta-ri — at.
at. We are the youth-ful guards-man of the pro-le-ta-ri — at.

WE AIN'T DOWN YET

PLEASE, MR BOSS

Key of C
Begins on G
Samuel H. Friedman
Quickly

Student Song
Arranged by
Dorothy Bachman

Wad-dya gon-na do when you want more pay, "Please, Mis-ter Boss?"
Wad-dya gon-na do when the scabs crawl in, "Please, Mis-ter Boss?"
Wad-dya gon-na do when the thugs get thick, "Please, Mis-ter Boss?"

Wad-dya gonna do for a short-er day, "Please Mis-ter Boss?"
Wad-dya gonna do when the spies be-gin, "Please Mis-ter Boss?"
Wad-dya gonna do when the cops come quick, "Please Mis-ter Boss?"

Wad-dya gonna do for a chance to play, "Please, Mis-ter Boss?" No! It's
Wad-dya gonna do when the gans-ters grin, "Please, Mis-ter Boss?" No! It's
Wad-dya gonna do when the judge gets slick, "Please Mis-ter Boss?" No! It's

strike, strike, strike, strike, strike, strike, strike. Not "Please Mis-ter Boss!"
stand, stand, stand, stand, stand, stand, stand. Not "Please Mis-ter Boss!"
fight, fight, fight, fight, fight, fight, fight. Not "Please Mis-ter Boss!"

MY LORD DELIBERED DANIEL

Key of F
Begins on C

Negro Spiritual
arranged by Dorothy Bachman

Stanzas 2,3,4 by Samuel H. Friedman

My Lord de-lib-ered Dan-iel My Lord delibered Dan-iel My Lord de-lib-ered Dan-iel Why can't he de-lib-er me?

1 I met a pil-grim on the way An' I ask him whar he's a-gwine. I'm
2 Oh Dan-iel cast in the li-on's den He pray both night and day. The
3 The Lord de-liv-ers ev'-ry man, that'll help the Lord a-long. So

bound for Ca-naan's hap-py lan', An' dis is de shout-ing band. Go on.
an-gel came from Gal-i-lee, An' took the li-on a-way. That's so
broth-ers lend a help-ing hand, As we shout our Dan-iel song. So strong

63

HEI-RO-JA-RUM

Key of F
Begins on C
Quickly

1. There was a rich man and he lived in Je-ru-sa-lem, Glory hal-le-lu-jah,
2. And at his gate there sat a hu-man wreck-i-um, Glory hal-le-lu-jah,
3. The poor man asked for a piece of bread and chees-i-um, Glory hal-le-lu-jah,
4. The poor man died and his soul went to heav-i-um, Glory hal-le-lu-jah,
5. The rich man died but he didn't fare so well-i-um, Glory hal-le-lu-jah,
6. Now the mor-al of this tale is that riches are no jok-i-um, Glory hal-le-lu-jah,

hei-ro-ja-rum. He wore a silk hat and his coat was very spruce-i-um Glo-ry hal-le-lu-jah
hei-ro-ja-rum. He wore a bowler hat and the rim was round his neck-i-um Glo-ry hal-le-lu-jah
hei-ro-ja-rum. The rich man said I'll call a po-li-ci-um Glo-ry hal-le-lu-jah
hei-ro-ja-rum. He danced with the saints till a quarter past e-lev-i-um Glo-ry hal-le-lu-jah
hei-ro-ja-rum. He couldn't go to heav'n so he had to go to hell-i-um Glo-ry hal-le-lu-jah
hei-ro-ja-rum. We'll all go to heav'n cause we're all stony brok-i-um Glo-ry hal-le-lu-jah

Cho.

hei - ro - ja - rum.
hei - ro - ja - rum.
hei - ro - ja - rum.
hei - ro - ja - rum.
hei - ro - ja - rum.
hei - ro - ja - rum.

Hei-ro-ja-rum, hei-ro-ja-rum, Skin-a-ma-link-a-doo-li-um,

skin-a-ma-link-a-doo-li-um, Glo-ry hal-le-lu-jah, hei-ro-ja-rum.

LET'S GET TOGETHER

Key of C
Begins on C
Langston Hughes

Carroll Tate

1. Who wants to come and join—hands with me?
2. Who wants to make one great and shin-ing land
3. Who wants to make a world that's real-ly fine?
4. Who wants to come and join—hands with me?

Who wants to make one great un-i-ty?
Where free-dom's call's meant for ev'-ry man?
Make your home-town a guid-ing light to shine?
Who wants to make one great un-i-ty?

Who wants to say "No more black or white"? Then
Who'll test the strength of the work-ers' might? Then
Who wants to lead work-ers to-ward light? Then
Who wants to say "No more black or white"? Then

let's get to-geth-er, folks, And fight, fight, fight!
let's get to-geth-er, folks, And fight, fight, fight!
let's get to-geth-er, folks, And fight, fight, fight!
let's get to-geth-er, folks, And fight, fight, fight!

GOD SAVE THE PEOPLE

Key of E minor
Begins on E
Ebenezer Elliott
Not too slowly

Josiah Booth

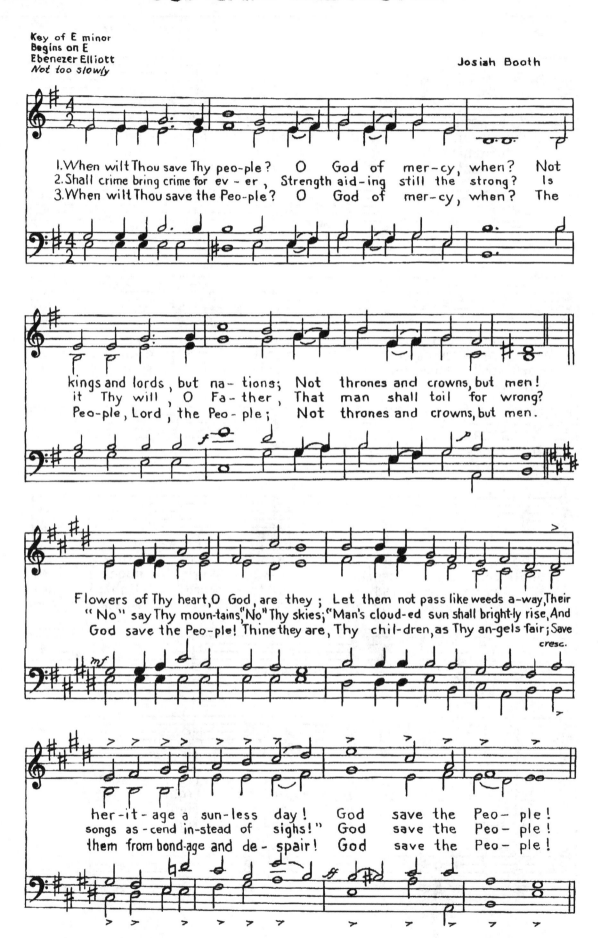

1. When wilt Thou save Thy peo-ple? O God of mer-cy, when? Not
2. Shall crime bring crime for ev - er, Strength aid-ing still the strong? Is
3. When wilt Thou save the Peo-ple? O God of mer-cy, when? The

kings and lords, but na - tions; Not thrones and crowns, but men!
it Thy will, O Fa-ther, That man shall toil for wrong?
Peo-ple, Lord, the Peo-ple; Not thrones and crowns, but men.

Flowers of Thy heart, O God, are they; Let them not pass like weeds a-way,Their
"No" say Thy moun-tains,"No" Thy skies;"Man's cloud-ed sun shall bright-ly rise, And
God save the Peo-ple! Thine they are, Thy chil-dren, as Thy an-gels fair; Save

cresc.

her-it-age a sun-less day! God save the Peo - ple!
songs as-cend in-stead of sighs!" God save the Peo - ple!
them from bond-age and de-spair! God save the Peo - ple!

WE COME

key of D
Begins on A

Edith Berkowitz   Edith Berkowitz

We come from out of the mills and shops: We come from out of the mines:

Sing-ing the songs of the work-ers' fight, Strong voic-es and lengthening lines.   Too

long we've served the boss-es, To make their lives com-plete They've re-fused to heed our suff'ring, But they'll

hear our march-ing feet! We come, the work-ers' red flag un-furled, We come to take back our world!

Awake, You Sleeping Workers

Key of Eb
Begins on Bb
Bill Wolff   Old German

A- wake you sleep-ing workers, the un-ion is call-ing: A-rise, a-rise, the

un-ion is call-ing; Get up! get up! get up! get up!

HARK! THE BATTLE CRY

Key of F
Begins on F

"Men of Harlech"
Welsh

H. S. Salt

March time.

1. Hark! the bat-tle cry is ring-ing! Hope with-in our bos-oms spring-ing, Bids us jour-ney for-ward sing-ing,
2. Long in wrath and des-per-a-tion, Long in hun-ger, shame, pri-va-tion, Have we born the deg-ra-da-tion,

Death to ty-rants' might! Tho we weild nor spear nor sa-bre, We the stur-dy sons of la-bor,
Of the rich man's spite. Now dis-dain-ing use-less sor-row, Hope from bright-er thoughts we'll bor-row;

Help-ing ev'-ry man his neigh-bor, Shrink not from the fight. See our homes be-fore us; Wives and babes im-
Oft-en shines the fair-est mor-row, Aft-er storm-iest night. Ty-rant hearts, take warn-ing, No-bler days are

Cho.

plore us   So firm we stand in heart and hand And swell the daunt-less cho-rus.   Men of la-bor
dawn-ing; He-ro-ic deeds, sub-lim-er creeds Shall her-ald free-dom's morn-ing!

young or hoar-y, Would ye win a name in sto-ry? Strike for home, for life, for glo-ry, Jus-tice, free-dom, right.

68

WE ARE LABOR

Key of G minor
Begins on G

Elizabeth Morgan

1. We who plant and reap the har-vest, toil-ing long be-neath the sun; We who mine in earth and dark-ness, We are la-bor: We are one. We who feed the fires un-dy-ing, We who gi-ant en-gines run, We who need-less swift are ply-ing We are la-bor We are one.

2. We are the un-end-ing pow-er By which world-wide work is done; Fill-ing man's each want each hour, We are la-bor: We are one. In each na-tion hope is bright'ning Where this truth is un-der-stood We, the work-ers, can u-nit-ing Bind the world in broth-er-hood.

Emancipation Day Song

Key of D
Begins on D

Traditional song from Texas
Contributed by Prentice Thomas
Arrang. by Elizabeth L. Morgan

Chorus

Free at last! Free at last! Thank God-a-mighty I'm free at last. Free at last! Free at last!

End here

Thank God-a-mighty I'm free at last! 1. If you get there be-fore I do —, Thank God-a-mighty I'm
2. One day as I was walk-ing a-long—, Thank God-a-might-y I'm

free at last, Tell all my friends I'm com-ing too —, Thank God-a-might-y I'm free at last.
free at last, My heart kept singing this joy-ful song—, Thank God-a-might-y I'm free at last.

THOTS ARE FREE

Key of B
Begins on F

Joyously

1. Our thots are all free, who, then shall con-fine them? Like sha-dows they flee; who shall see or di-vine them?
2. I think as I will the thots of my choos-ing, Well hid-den and still are the themes of my musing.
3. What tho I lie in pain in the som-ber-est pris-on? No fet-ter, no chain holds a spir-it a-ris-en;

No man can way lay them, no hun-ter can slay them 'Tis clear as can be that thot is still free.
My fan-cies, my yearn-ings, none mars by his spurn-ing. 'Tis clear as can be that thot is still free.
Dun-geon walls it will bat-ter, all shack-les 'twill shat-ter, Far & wide it will flee--- for thot is still free!

HYMN TO RIEGO

Key of F
Begins on C
Translation from the Spanish
by Nancy Head

Spanish Folk Song

1. Oh, joy - ous and fear-less, Au - da - cious, in - vin - ci - ble. Come
2. A - live is the glo - ry Of those who have strug-gled. The

sing with us com-rades Our might-y bat-tle song. For-ev - er re-
whole world re-mem-bers Their part in the strife. Ri - e - go, Ri-

mem-bered, A-dored by the mass-es, You brave sons of the work-ers And
e - go, We sing of your vic-tory. For the cause of the work-ers You

peas-ants of Spain. It is for our peo - ple, For Spain we must u
laid down your life.

Chorus

nite. For vic-to-ry and free-dom We'll win or die in the fight.

WE SHALL NOT BE MOVED

Key of G
Begins on B

Pentecostal Hymn

We shall not, We shall not be moved. We shall not, We shall not be moved. Just like a tree that's planted by the

wa — ter, We shall not be moved. The workers are in back of us, We shall not be moved

The workers are in back of us, We shall not be moved. Just like a tree that's plant-ed by the

wa — ter. We shall not be moved.

72

JAKIE AND ANDY

Key of C minor
Begins on C

Wm. Wolff

Wm. Wolff

Deliberately, with a marked rythm

Jak-ie and An-dy were two stin-gy boss-es, They sweat-ed their work-ers and talked of their loss-es, Till up rose the work-ers and went out on strike And said to the boss-es, "Oh your chis-el-ing we'll spike!" Poor Jak-ie! Poor An-dy! They said to the boss-es, "Oh your chis-el-ing we'll spike.

WHO'LL BUY

Key of G
Begins on G

Who'll buy my gray sand, Who'll buy my gray sand, Who'll buy my gray sand.

WHOSE ?

Key of D
Begins on D

Teresina Rowell

Teresina Rowell

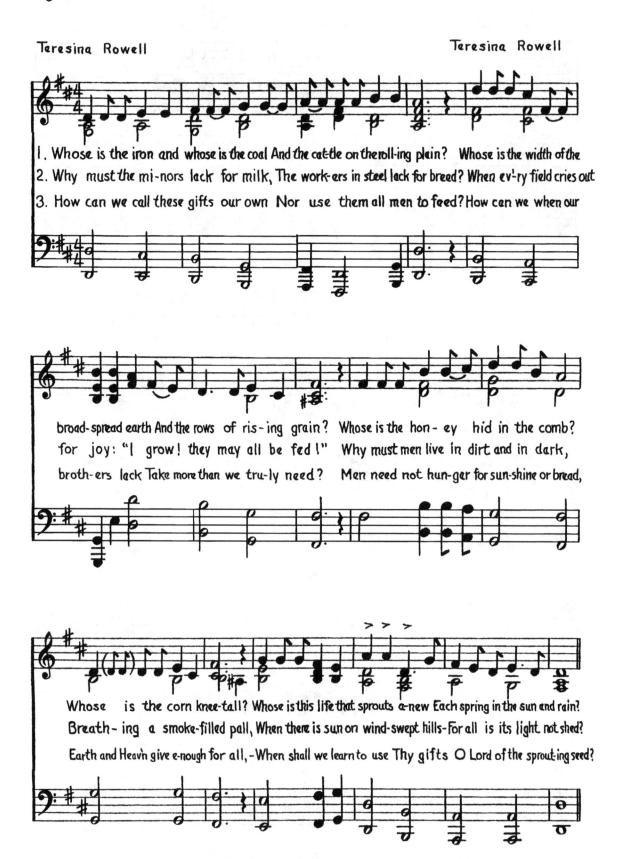

1. Whose is the iron and whose is the coal And the cat-tle on the roll-ing plain? Whose is the width of the

2. Why must the mi-nors lack for milk, The work-ers in steel lack for bread? When ev'-ry field cries out

3. How can we call these gifts our own Nor use them all men to feed? How can we when our

broad-spread earth And the rows of ris-ing grain? Whose is the hon- ey hid in the comb?

for joy: "I grow! they may all be fed!" Why must men live in dirt and in dark,

broth-ers lack Take more than we tru-ly need? Men need not hun-ger for sun-shine or bread,

Whose is the corn knee-tall? Whose is this life that sprouts a-new Each spring in the sun and rain?

Breath- ing a smoke-filled pall, When there is sun on wind-swept hills-For all is its light not shed?

Earth and Heav'n give e-nough for all, -When shall we learn to use Thy gifts O Lord of the sprout-ing seed?

THE CHAIN GANG

Key of F Minor
Begins on C

Russian Folk Song

1. The sun o'er the steppes now is set-ting, And far off is gild-ing the grass, And
2. They walk, heads all shav-en and hat-less, As thous-ands be-fore them have march'd, With
3. The shad-ows are length-en-ing ev-er; In dark-ness are wag-on and horse And
4. A voice then is heard in the dark-ness, "Brave broth-ers, be-tray not your gloom, The
5. They sing of the great moth-er Vol-ga— A might-y and glad-en-ing tune—Of
6. They sing of the steppes and their vast-ness, Of free-dom in deed and in word, Till

naught now is heard but the clank-ing of chains As the pris-on-ers pass.
brows that are fur-row'd in an-guish, With sore hearts and lips that are parch'd.
on-ly the guards can be heard now, Whose hearts feel no pain nor re-morse.
brave show self-mas-ter-y al-ways And nev-er are crushed by their doom."
days when they yet had their free-dom And vow "We'll be free a-gain soon!"
dark-ness has hid-den their an-guish And on-ly the chains can be heard.

Cling, clang, cling, clang, Pris'ners' chains are drag-ging. Cling, clang, cling, clang,

Wear-y steps are lag-ging. Cling, clang, cling, clang, Tolls the hope-less knell

As they lead our brav-est com-rades to Si-ber-ia's hell.

75

GO DOWN, MOSES

Key of E minor
Begins on B

Negro
Spiritual

Mournfully

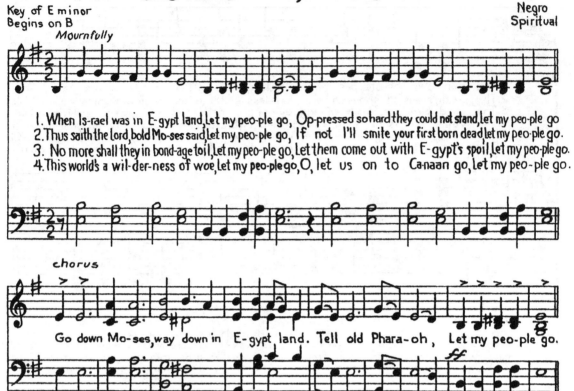

1. When Is-rael was in E-gypt land, Let my peo-ple go, Op-pressed so hard they could not stand, let my peo-ple go
2. Thus saith the Lord, bold Mo-ses said, Let my peo-ple go, If not I'll smite your first born dead, let my peo-ple go.
3. No more shall they in bond-age toil, Let my peo-ple go, Let them come out with E-gypt's spoil, let my peo-ple go.
4. This world's a wil-der-ness of woe, Let my peo-ple go, O, let us on to Ca-naan go, let my peo-ple go.

chorus

Go down Mo-ses, way down in E-gypt land. Tell old Phara-oh, Let my peo-ple go.

UP, SOCIALIST COMRADES

Key of F
Begins on C
Translated from the German
by Samuel H. Friedman

"Sozialisten march"
Carl Gramm
Arranged by
Dorothy Bachman

Up Socialist comrades, mass your numbers, The drums are beating, banners fly, For labor's hosts rise from their slumbers, And freedom's cause can never die! We fight to bring to all who toil, The beauty of the sun and soil, The might of knowledge and the splendor. When service to our class we render. This is the only war workers should fight, This is the only war workers will fight; Ours is the mass; Ours be the might. Ours is the mass; ours be the might!

- 2 -

Uncounted hosts throughout the nation,
   From shop and office, mill and field,
Whose toil means sorrow and starvation,
   Learn that the power is yours to wield.
Have done with sighing and with tears;
Close ranks, the hour of freedom nears.
All exploitation we shall banish,
War, waste and want at last will vanish.
This is the only war workers should fight.
This is the only war workers will fight.
Ours is the mass, Ours be the might.
Ours is the mass, Ours be the might.

THE WORKERS HYMN

Key of Eb
Begins on G

Translation by Samuel H. Friedman

Italian Worker's Song

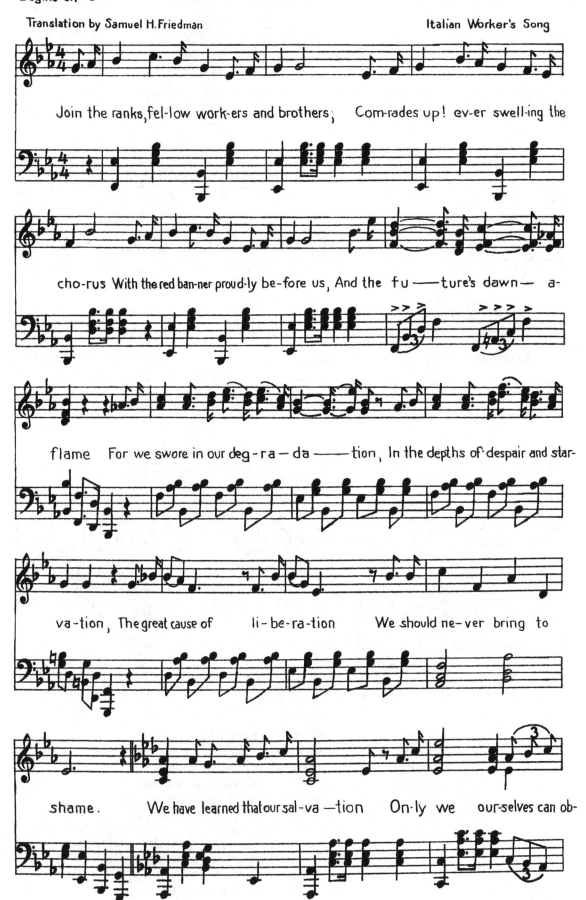

Join the ranks, fel-low work-ers and brothers; Com-rades up! ev-er swell-ing the

cho-rus With the red ban-ner proud-ly be-fore us, And the fu——ture's dawn— a-

flame For we swore in our deg-ra-da———tion, In the depths of despair and star-

va-tion, The great cause of li-be-ra-tion We should ne-ver bring to

shame. We have learned that our sal-va—tion On-ly we our-selves can ob-

tain ———. We shall con ——— quer for the toil———ers or fight

on 'till we are slain ———. We shall bat—tle a-gainst the de-

spoil ———ers, And our mar-tyrs shall not have died in

vain———. We shall con-quer for the toil—ers Or fight

on ——————— till we are slain ! 'Till we are slain !

THE OLD FARM HOME

Key of G
Begins on D

Swing it

"The Old Grey Mare"

1. Oh, the old farm home, it ain't what it used to be, Mort-gaged from A to Z, What fun for you and me The
2. Oh, the poor old farm-er ain't what he used to be, All full of mis-er-y, Broke as he can be. The
3. Oh, the poor old cow, she ain't what she used to be, Thin as a punk-in seed, Ain't had no oats nor feed. The
4. Oh, the poor old horse, he ain't what he used to be, All of his ribs we see, Man-gy and full of fleas. The
5. Oh, the old ma-chin-ery that is no long-er mine Bust-ed and tied in line, With wire & bind-er twine. The
6. Oh, the Un-ion Jun-iors, in clear up to their necks, Clean-in up such a wreck—That's what we'll do by heck! The

old farm home, it ain't what it used to be, Ma-ny long years a-go.　　Ma-ny long years a-go,
poor old farm-er ain't what he used to be, Ma-ny long years a-go.　　Ma-ny long years a-go,
poor old cow, she ain't what she used to be, Ma-ny long years a-go.　　Ma-ny long years a-go,
poor old horse, he ain't what he used to be, Ma-ny long years a-go.　　Ma-ny long years a-go,

old ma-chin-ery ain't what it used to be, Ma-ny long years a-go.　　Ma-ny long years a-go,
Un-ion Jun-iors, in clear up to their necks, We're gonna make things go!　We're gon-na make things go!

Ma-ny long years a-go. The old farm home, it ain't what it used to be, Ma-ny long years a-go.
Ma-ny long years a-go. The poor old farm-er ain't what he used to be, Ma-ny long years a-go.
Ma-ny long years a-go. The poor old cow, she ain't what she used to be, Ma-ny long years a-go.
Ma-ny long years a-go. The poor old horse, he ain't what he used to be, Ma-ny long years a-go.

Ma-ny long years a-go. The old ma-chin-ery ain't what it used to be, Ma-ny long years a-go.
Sure gon-na make things go. The Un-ion Jun-iors, we'll do the job, you bet! Wh'd you say gang let's go.

About PM Press

PM Press was founded at the end of 2007 by a small collection of folks with decades of publishing, media, and organizing experience. PM Press co-conspirators have published and distributed hundreds of books, pamphlets, CDs, and DVDs. Members of PM have founded enduring book fairs, spearheaded victorious tenant organizing campaigns, and worked closely with bookstores, academic conferences, and even rock bands to deliver political and challenging ideas to all walks of life. We're old enough to know what we're doing and young enough to know what's at stake.

We seek to create radical and stimulating fiction and nonfiction books, pamphlets, T-shirts, visual and audio materials to entertain, educate, and inspire you. We aim to distribute these through every available channel with every available technology, whether that means you are seeing anarchist classics at our bookfair stalls; reading our latest vegan cookbook at the café; downloading geeky fiction e-books; or digging new music and timely videos from our website.

Contact us for direct ordering and questions about all PM Press releases, as well as manuscript submissions, review copy requests, foreign rights sales, author interviews, to book an author for an event, and to have PM Press attend your bookfair:

PM Press • PO Box 23912 • Oakland, CA 94623
510-658-3906 • info@pmpress.org

Buy books and stay on top of what we are doing at:

www.pmpress.org

FOPM

MONTHLY SUBSCRIPTION PROGRAM

These are indisputably momentous times—the financial system is melting down globally and the Empire is stumbling. Now more than ever there is a vital need for radical ideas.

In the six years since its founding—and on a mere shoestring—PM Press has risen to the formidable challenge of publishing and distributing knowledge and entertainment for the struggles ahead. With over 250 releases to date, we have published an impressive and stimulating array of literature, art, music, politics, and culture. Using every available medium, we've succeeded in connecting those hungry for ideas and information to those putting them into practice.

Friends of PM allows you to directly help impact, amplify, and revitalize the discourse and actions of radical writers, filmmakers, and artists. It provides us with a stable foundation from which we can build upon our early successes and provides a much-needed subsidy for the materials that can't necessarily pay their own way. You can help make that happen—and receive every new title automatically delivered to your door once a month—by joining as a Friend of PM Press. And, we'll throw in a free T-shirt when you sign up.

Here are your options:

- $30 a month: Get all books and pamphlets plus 50% discount on all webstore purchases
- $40 a month: Get all PM Press releases (including CDs and DVDs) plus 50% discount on all webstore purchases
- $100 a month: Superstar—Everything plus PM merchandise, free downloads, and 50% discount on all webstore purchases

For those who can't afford $35 or more a month, we're introducing **Sustainer Rates** at $15, $10 and $5. Sustainers get a free PM Press T-shirt and a 50% discount on all purchases from our website.

Your Visa or Mastercard will be billed once a month, until you tell us to stop. Or until our efforts succeed in bringing the revolution around. Or the financial meltdown of Capital makes plastic redundant. Whichever comes first.

REBEL VOICES
An IWW Anthology

Edited by Joyce L. Kornbluh
Preface by Daniel Gross
Contributions by Franklin Rosemont
Introduction by Fred Thompson
$27.95 • 472 Pages • 10 by 7
ISBN: 978-1-60486-483-0

Welcoming women, Blacks, and immigrants long before most other unions, the Wobblies from the start were labor's outstanding pioneers and innovators, unionizing hundreds of thousands of workers previously regarded as "unorganizable." Wobblies organized the first sit-down strike (at General Electric, Schenectady, 1906), the first major auto strike (6,000 Studebaker workers, Detroit, 1911), the first strike to shut down all three coalfields in Colorado (1927), and the first "no-fare" transit-workers' job-action (Cleveland, 1944). With their imaginative, colorful, and world-famous strikes and free-speech fights, the IWW wrote many of the brightest pages in the annals of working class emancipation.

Wobblies also made immense and invaluable contributions to workers' culture. All but a few of America's most popular labor songs are Wobbly songs. IWW cartoons have long been recognized as labor's finest and funniest.

The impact of the IWW has reverberated far beyond the ranks of organized labor. An important influence on the 1960s New Left, the Wobbly theory and practice of direct action, solidarity, and "class-war" humor have inspired several generations of civil rights and antiwar activists, and are a major source of ideas and inspiration for today's radicals. Indeed, virtually every movement seeking to "make this planet a good place to live" (to quote an old Wobbly slogan), has drawn on the IWW's incomparable experience.

Originally published in 1964 and long out of print, *Rebel Voices* remains by far the biggest and best source on IWW history, fiction, songs, art, and lore. This new edition includes 40 pages of additional material from the 1998 Charles H. Kerr edition from Fred Thompson and Franklin Rosemont, and a new preface by Wobbly organizer Daniel Gross.

> The IWW blazed a path in industrial history and its influence is still felt today. Joyce Kornbluh has performed a valuable service to unionism by compiling this comprehensive anthology on the more militant side of labor history."
> —*Southwest Labor*

THE WORLD TURNED UPSIDE DOWN
Rosselsongs 1960–2010

Leon Rosselson
$44.95 • 4xCD • 240 Minutes and 80 Pages
ISBN: 978-1-60486-498-4

The life and times of England's greatest living songwriter are captured in a deluxe box set, containing 72 songs on 4 CDs and an 80-page book.

"The songs on these CDs span 5 decades, from the sparky sixties to the curdled present, and encompass a wide variety of song subjects and song forms. They have been written out of hope, anger, love, scorn, laughter and despair. The tracks I have selected are, I believe, sturdily built and quite capable of standing up for themselves. And, because they have something to say about the times in which they were written, there are copious notes on the political and personal environments that formed them along with some pointed observations on the craft of songwriting."
—Leon Rosselson

Frankie Armstrong, Roy Bailey, Mark Bassey, Steve Berry, Billy Bragg, Martin Carthy, Howard Evans, Clare Lintott, Chris Foster, Sue Harris, Paul Jayasinha, Sianed Jones, John Kirkpatrick, Elizabeth Mansfield, Ruth Rosselson, Fiz Shapur, Dave Swarbrick, Miranda Sykes, Roger Williams, The 3 City 4, The Oyster Band, and The Sheffield Socialist Choir all contribute variously to the songs too, in one form or another.

THE LIBERTY TREE
A Celebration of the Life and Writings of Thomas Paine

Leon Rosselson and Robb Johnson
$20.00 • 2xCD • 120 Minutes and 20 Pages
ISBN: 978-1-60486-339-0

The Liberty Tree tells the story of Tom Paine's extraordinary life, interweaving Paine's own words, from his letters and the pamphlets which made him one of the most influential and dangerous writers of his age, with extracts from newspaper reports, diaries, letters and other documents of the times. The songs of Robb Johnson and Leon Rosselson add another dimension to the story, reflecting Paine's radical ideas and evaluating them in the context of the 21st century. This unique blend of words and music challenges received opinion in the same way Paine's writings did.

MAKING SPEECH FREE

Utah Phillips
$14.95 • CD • 74 Minutes
ISBN: 978-1-60486-355-0

"As it happened, most of my greatest teachers were or had been members of the Industrial Workers of the World, the Wobblies. That's why I became one over forty years ago. These old Wobs showed me a way to get through the world without giving away my mind, body, and soul to a bunch of witless tyrants who only want cheap labor that can be thrown away when they don't need it anymore. These songs weren't learned from books or records, but from sitting in front of live people and saying, 'Sing that again,' until I finally got it. These stories, polemics, and rants grew out of years of asking questions, listening closely, and trying out what I heard on the world around me. I guess that part of growing up is finally deciding what you authentically inherit, what was it that was passed along to you by our elders. Then it's our turn to keep it in the world by passing it along. So here it is. Some of it, anyway."
—Utah Phillips

Captured live on May 7, 1999, as part of a Free Speech Teach-In, the inestimable "Golden Voice of the Great Southwest," delivers 74 minutes of his trademark history, humor, song, and struggle in a signature performance. Utah's songs and stories remind us to "Don't Mourn, Organize," and that we can be inspired, educated, and entertained while we do it.

ENGLISH REBEL SONGS 1381–1984
Chumbawamba
$14.95 • CD • 42 Minutes
ISBN: 978-1-60486-000-9

English Rebel Songs 1381–1984 is Chumbawamba's homage to the men and women who never had obituaries in the broadsheets; those who never received titles or appeared in as an entry in "Who's Who." This is an album that conjures up the tragedies and triumphs of the people who shaped England: its citizens. This album was originally recorded in 1988 when Chumbawamba was determined to stir up a rout in the tiny anarcho-punk community by swapping guitars and drums for a cappella singing. The songs were discovered in songbooks, in folk clubs and on cassette tapes, chopped and changed and bludgeoned into shape with utmost respect for the original tunes. Fierce, sweet, and powerful, *English Rebel Songs 1381–1984* contains ballads not included on the original album. It's guaranteed to sway the listener, break hearts, and encourage hope . . . just as those who inspired the songs by changing history.

SONGS OF FREEDOM
The James Connolly Songbook

James Connolly
Edited by Mat Callahan with a Preface by Theo Dorgan and a Foreword by James Connolly Heron
$12.95 • 9 by 6 • 96 Pages • ISBN: 978-1-60486-826-5

Songs of Freedom is the name of the songbook edited by James Connolly and published in 1907. Connolly's introduction is better known than the collection for which it was written, containing his oft-quoted maxim: "Until the movement is marked by the joyous, defiant singing of revolutionary songs, it lacks one of the most distinctive marks of a popular revolutionary movement, it is the dogma of a few and not the faith of the multitude." Though most of the songs were of Irish derivation, the songbook itself was published in New York and directed to the American working class, explicitly internationalist in its aims.

Songs of Freedom is a celebration of the life and work of James Connolly, the Irish revolutionary socialist martyred by the British government for his role in the Easter Rising of 1916. It is at once a collection of stirring revolutionary songs and a vital historical document. For the first time in a hundred years, readers will find the original *Songs of Freedom* as well as the *1919 Connolly Souvenir* program published in Dublin for a concert commemorating Connolly's birth. Both are reproduced exactly as they originally appeared, providing a fascinating glimpse of the workers' struggle at the beginning of the last century. To complete the picture is included the *James Connolly Songbook* of 1972, which contains not only the most complete selection of Connolly's lyrics, but also historical background essential to understanding the context in which the songs were written and performed.

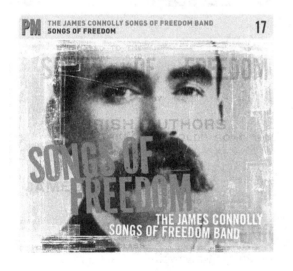

SONGS OF FREEDOM

The James Connolly Songs of Freedom Band
$14.95 • CD • 53 Minutes
ISBN: 978-1-60486-831-9

From the rollicking welcome of "A Festive Song" to the defiant battle cry of "Watchword of Labor," *Songs of Freedom* accomplishes the difficult task of making contemporary music out of old revolutionary songs. Far from the archival preservation of embalmed corpses, the inspired performance of a rocking band turns the timeless lyrics of James Connolly into timely manifestos for today's young rebels. As Connolly himself repeatedly urged, nothing can replace the power of music to raise the fighting spirit of the oppressed.

Giving expression to Connolly's internationalism, musical influences ranging from traditional Irish airs to American rhythm and blues are combined here in refreshing creativity.

CPSIA information can be obtained
at www.ICGtesting.com
Printed in the USA
JSHW032120090921
18523JS00006B/10